Simple Ideas

A GUIDE TO EVERYDAY COOKING WITH THERMOMIX®

thermomix

DEAR CUSTOMER,

Welcome to the exciting, creative and delicious world of Thermomix®.

We believe that the value of a good meal comes from much more than simply the act of eating it. Food brings families and friends together. It helps to forge connections, build relationships and create lasting memories. Food is the cornerstone of our lives and with Thermomix®, good food is simply easier.

This book is your guide to cooking the Thermomix® way. We've selected recipes that showcase the innovative and creative functionality of Thermomix®, while demonstrating the various ways it can save you time and money. Alongside a selection of recipes for all occasions, you'll find specific chapters focused on different areas; from quick, everyday cooking, to recipes that will wow. We've also included general kitchen organisation tips, meal-planning advice and solutions for feeding a family.

All the recipes in this book are available on your Thermomix®. There are also thousands more recipes from all over the world on our online recipe platform Cookidoo®, providing you with endless culinary inspiration.

And, when you want to enhance your cooking abilities and learn new skills, take a look at one of our exciting cooking masterclasses or get online and discover the support of our friendly communities.

Whether you're a novice in the kitchen or an experienced cook, we hope Thermomix® inspires you to embark on your own cooking journey.

Happy cooking,

Caroline Snook
Recipe Development Manager, Thermomix® UK and Ireland

Contents

Introduction

Welcome to Your New Lifestyle

Cooking is a part of life. With Thermomix® to help you, preparing nutritious and satisfying meals for you and your family will be easier than ever before. However, a recipe is just the start – cooking is about so much more than simply getting food onto a plate. With Thermomix®, we hope you'll discover the great pleasure of spending time in the kitchen preparing a meal and the joy of sitting down with friends and family to enjoy it together.

SIMPLE, EFFICIENT, CREATIVE AND FUN

COOKING FROM SCRATCH
Healthy

Thermomix® makes light work of preparing homemade store cupboard or fridge staples. By making your own, you'll know exactly what is going into the meals you eat – natural ingredients without preservatives, with less sugar and, when necessary, no allergens. Try making your own sauces, yoghurts, biscuits, jams and juices, and **discover a more natural way of eating.**

FREEDOM IN THE KITCHEN
Creative

Be the chef you want to be! There's no need to wait for a family get together to enjoy your Grandma's apple pie, or pop to the shops because you're out of mayonnaise, or even order a takeaway for pizza night with the kids. And who says you need to be a professional chef to create delicious meals that will impress your friends? Whether you follow a recipe or break away from the rules and get creative, one thing is certain; **with Thermomix®, you can achieve anything.**

LIVING IN THE MOMENT
Time saving

With the hectic pace of modern life, free time is one of life's great luxuries. After a long, tiring day, often the last thing you want is to spend all evening cooking, and that is where Thermomix® comes in – it saves you time, freeing you up to do other things. Meal preparation is much quicker, with basic tasks such as chopping onions done in seconds. In addition, the cooking and stirring functions mean you can leave Thermomix® to prepare your meal, safe in the knowledge it will be cooked to perfection.

HELP IN THE KITCHEN, AND AWAY FROM IT
Easy

With Thermomix®, you can cook following step-by-step instructions, view photos and videos of recipes and navigate through Cookidoo®, our online recipe platform. By tapping the screen, you can start cooking, search for dinner ideas, plan the week's menu, write your shopping list and more. Even better, when it comes to searching for recipe inspiration or making your shopping list, you don't need to be in your kitchen. Thermomix® recipes and features travel with you anywhere, via your computer, tablet or smartphone, making mealtimes easier when you don't have the time to plan ahead.

LESS SHOPPING, LESS WASTE
Money saving

There are some things that you'll never want to buy again after making them in your Thermomix®. Not only are they tastier and easier to prepare, but they also save you money. Sauces, spice mixes, yoghurts, cheeses, smoothies, soups, cookies and birthday cakes are just a few examples. In addition, you have complete control over your ingredients and subsequently, your food waste. Add vegetable stalks to a morning smoothie; make fruit juice with peel and still achieve a smooth texture; turn the leftovers in the fridge into a delicious quiche in minutes; freeze a surplus of ripe fruit for ice cream and milkshakes. Less shopping, less waste, more savings.

Have you ever wanted to bake a special cake for a loved one's birthday, but weren't sure where to start? Or prepare a dinner party menu that would really impress your friends?

Next time you need a little help in the kitchen, this book, together with your Thermomix®, will come to the rescue.

APPLIANCE FEATURES

TOUCHSCREEN
Just like a tablet with WiFi
The touchscreen enables you to access all features and cooking modes, and connect directly to Cookidoo®.

COOKIDOO®
Thousands of Thermomix® recipes with guaranteed success
With Cookidoo® membership, your kitchen is always connected to our online recipe platform. Search thousands of tested recipes, view photos and recipe videos, and start cooking right away. With recipes to suit every occasion, you'll never be short of ideas.

SMARTER COOKING
Let Thermomix® do the work
With Guided Cooking recipes, you have step-by-step cooking instructions. Time, temperature and speed functions are all preset; Thermomix® will start the cooking and prompt you for the next ingredient. You can relax and carry on a conversation while preparing dinner – don't worry, you won't miss a step!

COOK ON FOUR LEVELS
Prepare several dishes at once
Imagine cooking a soup and side dish at the same time as you're preparing the main course. Discover how to cook using multiple levels: the mixing bowl, simmering basket, Varoma dish and Varoma tray. Convenient, fast and energy efficient.

HIGH-TEMPERATURE COOKING
For more intense flavours
The high-temperature cooking mode allows extra browning and creates more intense flavours, while making caramel, a cooking process that's feared by many, is made easy.

RELIABLE QUALITY
Cook with confidence
The high precision and durability of Thermomix® makes it the most reliable kitchen assistant. When you can be absolutely sure that a risotto will come out perfectly and a sauce won't have lumps or curdle, cooking becomes a joy. With precise temperature control, the possibilities are endless when cooking with Thermomix®.

CLEVER ACCESSORIES
Easy and useful
The spatula is designed to minimise waste, the butterfly whisk whips cream and whisks egg whites perfectly, the simmering basket allows you to cook eggs or strain lemonade... Thermomix® and its different parts have all been designed to make your cooking experience even easier.

Your Thermomix®

Your Thermomix® comes fully equipped with everything you need to carry out the functions of more than twelve kitchen appliances.

Varoma
The Thermomix® Varoma provides a gentle, easy way to steam vegetables, meats, fish, fruits, cakes and breads.

Mixing bowl lid
An integral part of the built-in safety measures, the lid must be in place for the locking arms to close around it and for Thermomix® to start. Also useful when making emulsified sauces such as mayonnaise, oil can be drizzled onto the lid to drip into the mixing bowl at the perfect speed.

Mixing knife
The efficient, multi-purpose mixing knife is the heart of Thermomix®. Just one knife stirs at low speeds, mixes at medium speeds (2-4) and chops or grinds at higher speeds. In addition, the reverse function can be selected for more gentle stirring or shredding.

Simmering basket
Food cooked in the simmering basket is held clear of the rotating knife for perfect steaming or boiling and the lid closes over it, for additional safety.

All Thermomix® parts, except the main appliance, **are dishwasher safe.**

Varoma lid

Varoma tray

Varoma

Splash guard

Measuring cup

Mixing bowl lid

Butterfly whisk

Simmering basket

Mixing bowl

Mixing knife

Spatula
Shaped to work perfectly with the Thermomix® mixing bowl, the spatula is also used to easily remove the simmering basket.

Butterfly whisk
A versatile attachment used to aerate sauces and mousses, whisk egg whites, whip cream or make homemade butter.

Splash guard
A guard to protect against splashing of hot contents when cooking at higher temperatures.

Measuring cup
Used to close the hole in the mixing bowl lid, the measuring cup is also a handy 100 ml measure.

Mixing bowl
Thermomix® has a durable stainless steel mixing bowl with integrated heating.

Scales
In-built digital weighing scales ensure precision and accuracy with every recipe.

Heating system
An efficient heating system ensures the highest standard of performance when cooking with Thermomix®.

VORWERK

thermomix

Spatula

The Thermomix® World Goes Beyond Cooking

Imagine you're about to buy a new home. After extensive searching, you find the perfect place for you and your family. It's not just the house; it's the friendly neighbours, the local butchers and the park around the corner. It's more than just a home, it's a community.

Your Thermomix® is no different. It's your introduction to a community of like-minded users, all with a passion for cooking.

THERE'S ALWAYS SOMEONE TO HELP YOU

Your Thermomix® **Advisor** is on hand to assist you as and when you need it. Contact them whenever you need advice or have any questions about Thermomix®. You can also visit our **shops** to access specialised technical assistance, attend cooking classes and purchase Thermomix® accessories. In addition, our friendly **Customer Care** team are at the end of the phone for any technical help.

DIGITAL RECIPES FOR ENDLESS INSPIRATION

Cookidoo®, the Thermomix® online recipe platform, is continuously updated with new recipe suggestions. Explore this huge digital cookbook and find recipe ideas that will satisfy whoever you're feeding. With Cookidoo® membership, thousands of recipes are available, success-guaranteed, either directly on your Thermomix® or on your computer, tablet or smartphone – wherever you are.

COOKING EVENTS AND CLASSES TO SUPPORT YOU

Would you like to learn new cooking skills, tips and recipes? In our cooking classes, you will discover how to really make the most of your Thermomix®. What makes these classes special is the chance to sample select, new recipes and share experiences with fellow Thermomix® owners that will bring more value to your everyday cooking. Simply book a place at your local class and look forward to learning some new skills.

COOKBOOKS TO READ AT YOUR LEISURE

There's nothing like curling up with a good book. Our beautifully-presented Thermomix® cookbooks

are full of everything from everyday lunches to show-stopping dinner party centrepieces. Packed with recipes, cooking tips, nutritional information and articles written specifically for Thermomix®, our official Thermomix® recipe developers publish new titles every year. We hope they continue to enthuse you to turn on your Thermomix® and cook something new.

A COMMUNITY TO SUPPORT YOU

The Thermomix® Recipe Community is a meeting space where thousands of enthusiasts share their recipes and experiences. Here you can publish your own successful recipes and find helpful suggestions that others have shared. There is also a forum to ask questions and receive advice from experienced Thermomix® users.

FIND MORE ONLINE

Come and join the conversation! Share your passion for Thermomix®, your cooking experiences and your finished dishes with thousands of others on our official Thermomix® social media channels.

- ThermomixUK
  ThermomixIrelandOfficial
- @thermomixuk
- @UKThermomix
  @ThermomixIre
- Vorwerk Thermomix UK

Don't forget you can also visit our online store to purchase cookbooks and additional accessories to enhance your Thermomix® experience.

Thermomix®
Fits Your Lifestyle

Modern lives are constantly changing. Whether it's buying a new home, starting a new job, raising a family or travelling - adaptation is key. With Thermomix®, the ability to prepare healthy, home-cooked meals will remain a constant throughout.

Cookidoo® is the meal planning tool that is with you at all times, whether on the Thermomix® screen, your computer, tablet or smartphone. It adapts to the different needs of each user; from those who only cook occasionally, to those who need daily inspiration as well as for those who like to improvise using the ingredients they have at home.

ASK COOKIDOO®
"WHAT'S FOR DINNER?"

WHATEVER'S IN THE FRIDGE

Only have eggs or courgettes? Search according to the ingredients you have in the fridge or pantry and Cookidoo® will provide some meal solutions.

SOMETHING TO SUIT YOUR GUESTS

Got a dinner party tonight and only just found out that one of your guests is vegetarian? Use the category search and filters and in no time at all you'll have a variety of recipes to choose from that not only meet their dietary needs, but fit in with the time you have for meal preparation.

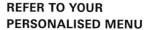

TRY OUR RECOMMENDATIONS

Not in the mood to search? No problem. Refer to the weekly suggestions on Cookidoo® or be inspired by other users and try out the recipes they've marked as their favourites.

REFER TO YOUR PERSONALISED MENU

Plan meals in advance and make a shopping list on Cookidoo®. The food shop can be done in one go which will save you time and money, and there'll be no more panic about what to make for dinner each night. By getting ahead, you'll know exactly what's on the menu.

CHECK OUT YOUR LISTS

You can group recipes into lists according to your needs, such as "Must try", "Meals in 30 minutes", or "Dad's birthday party". This way you'll always know where to find your favourite recipes, making meal-planning even easier.

Cookidoo® membership will provide you with endless inspiration. Don't forget all recipes are also available in Guided Cooking format, helping you get the most out of your Thermomix®.

Cooking with Thermomix®

Imagine coming home after a busy day and being able to quickly prepare a delicious meal with minimal effort. Cook up a pasta sauce in minutes, heat up a bowl of warming soup, recreate Grandma's tea-loaf, or wow your friends with a fancy dessert. You don't need to be a professional chef to follow a Guided Cooking recipe; successful results are guaranteed.

Enjoy cooking with Thermomix® – it's all of this and much more.

EVERYTHING YOU NEED IN ONE PLACE

Thermomix® replaces a long list of kitchen appliances and utensils; a timer, a mincer, a grater, a dough maker, a yoghurt maker, a kettle, a coffee and spice grinder, a juicer, a blender, a pestle and mortar, a mixer, a food processor, a steamer and scales. It's more than 12 functions integrated in one single appliance.

STIRRING

ON SPEED ⟲ TO 1

Let the Thermomix® mixing knife stir the ingredients continuously for even heat distribution and perfectly cooked dishes – without having to stand over a pan on the hob.

MIXING
ON SPEEDS 3-5

Mixing with Thermomix® is quick and easy, taking just a few seconds to mix a batter or sauce.

EMULSIFYING

ON SPEEDS 4-5

With Thermomix®, creating a perfectly emulsified salad dressing or mayonnaise is child's play. (See Sauces Masterclass p. 56.)

CHOPPING
ON SPEEDS 4-6

Perfectly chopped ingredients in seconds: the powerful Thermomix® chops onions, nuts, herbs, meat, carrots, potatoes and so much more. (See Resources p. 223.)

Grate 1000 g potatoes in 5 seconds or 1000 g onions in 4 seconds. Seeing is believing for this one!

BLENDING
ON SPEEDS 6-10

Achieve a perfectly blended texture for healthy smoothies, silky soups or fabulous cocktails. To blend, use speed 6 or higher for a few seconds if you prefer a chunky consistency, or longer for a smooth texture. When blending hot preparations, always increase the speed gradually.

GRINDING AND MILLING
ON SPEEDS 9-10

The powerful Thermomix® motor and high-quality mixing knife grinds or mills nuts, grains, sugar or Parmesan to the finest powder. (See Resources p. 223.)

COOKING

The Thermomix® mixing bowl is used for more than just mixing; it replaces your stainless steel saucepan, conducting heat efficiently to the

WHIPPING AND WHISKING WITH THE BUTTERFLY WHISK

You can whip cream in seconds or whisk egg whites quickly and easily. Insert the butterfly whisk on top of the mixing knife and set the speed to 2-4 (maximum).

ingredients within. Warming, heating, cooking or sautéing – Thermomix® cooks using precise heat and stirring settings, guaranteeing perfect results.

HEATING DELICATE PREPARATIONS BETWEEN 37-95°C

Integrated sensors within the mixing bowl regulate the temperature accurately and precisely. This is ideal for trickier preparations such as melting chocolate without burning, or making homemade yoghurt.

STEAMING

Steam a wide variety of ingredients in the Varoma dish, tray and simmering basket (see Resources p. 223). When steaming in the Varoma, you can also prepare a soup or stew in the mixing bowl at the same time. All the juices from the contents of the Varoma drip down into the preparation below, adding flavour and nutrients.
(See Multi-level Cooking Masterclass p. 134.)

WEIGHING

Having built-in scales allows for precision without effort, a transformative experience for new Thermomix® users. When you add ingredients to the mixing bowl, Thermomix® weighs them for you, then carries on with the recipe. Easy and minimum washing up!

KNEADING

The dough mode imitates the kneading action of a professional baker with an intermittent clockwise-counter-clockwise motion. Pizza dough can be kneaded in 2 minutes, with minimal effort and without getting your hands messy.

COOKING YOUR WAY

There are two ways to cook with Thermomix®; by yourself, or with extra help. Regardless of which one you choose, Thermomix® gives you the ability to make delicious and satisfying meals from scratch.

1

CLASSIC THERMOMIX® COOKING: YOU SET THE TIME, TEMPERATURE AND SPEED

With only three settings: time, temperature and speed, Thermomix® can perform many functions, eliminating the effort required in

traditional cooking. Classic Thermomix® cooking gives you full control over your dishes and allows you to adapt or create your own recipes with complete freedom.

START COOKING

Placing ingredients in a clean, dry mixing bowl ensures the best results for grinding and chopping, and is essential for whisking egg whites.

Time, temperature and speed are all displayed on one screen. The current setting is always highlighted and can easily be adjusted by turning the dial.

HOW TO USE DIFFERENT TEMPERATURES AND SPEEDS

Temperatures
In classic Thermomix® cooking, choose temperatures between 37°C and 120°C:

- **37-55°C:** melt or warm gently (e.g. chocolate).
- **60-80°C:** cook gently, similar to a bain-marie (e.g. sauces, custard).
- **80-95°C:** heat milk without over-boiling or water (e.g. for speciality tea).
- **100°C:** boil water or cook (e.g. soups, stews).
- **105-115°C:** cook (e.g. sugar syrup).
- **120°C:** sauté (e.g. onions).
- **Varoma:** steam (e.g. fish, breads).

Thermomix® can also reach higher temperatures in Guided Cooking recipes.

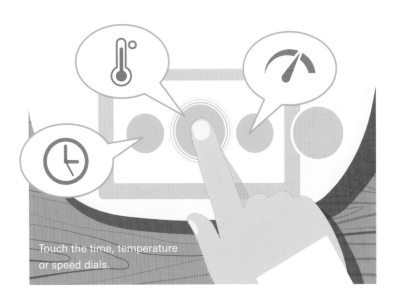

Touch the time, temperature or speed dials.

Speeds

- **Speed ⌀:** stir as if you were mixing using a wooden spoon (e.g. risotto).
- **Speed 1-3:** mix gently, mash potatoes or chop soft ingredients (e.g. hard boiled eggs, raw mushrooms).
- **Speed 4-6:** chop (e.g. onions, carrots), emulsify (e.g. mayonnaise).
- **Speed 7-10** and **Turbo:** grind or mill (e.g. sugar, wheat, coffee), blend to a completely smooth texture (e.g. creamy soups, smoothies, ice creams) or chop hard ingredients (e.g. cured ham, hard cheeses).
- **Reverse ↻ with low speeds** (⌀ to 3) will prevent delicate foods from falling apart (e.g. risotto).
- **Reverse ↻ with speed 4** can be used for shredding ingredients without chopping them (e.g. pulled pork).

Modes

A mode is an automated function that allows Thermomix® to handle a specific task for you.

For instance, the **Warm up mode** lets you gently reheat your leftovers. Use the **Kettle mode** to heat up water for a cup of tea, or milk for your breakfast. You choose the temperature and Thermomix® will heat it precisely for you. **Cleaning** makes washing up after dinner a quick and painless process. The **Scales** let you measure ingredients precisely into the mixing bowl or into another container. **Turbo** operates Thermomix® at maximum speed, in short bursts. When making breads or pizza doughs, **Dough mode** imitates the kneading action of a professional baker.

Swipe the home screen to access these and **many other modes**. You'll find further explanations for each one by touching its information icon on your Thermomix®.

We are constantly programming **new modes** to make our customers' lives easier. So, keep an eye out for the latest updates!

Place approx. 1000 g water and a few drops of washing up liquid in the mixing bowl and start Cleaning mode.

2

GUIDED COOKING: ALL PRESET FOR YOU

To make things even easier, follow a Guided Cooking recipe. Simply select a recipe from Cookidoo® and follow the steps on screen.

Advanced dishes are made easy with Guided Cooking and even the most inexperienced cooks will be preparing dishes they never would have thought possible.

Guided Cooking also lets you cook at higher temperatures, for example when caramelising onions, browning meat or making caramel. For Thermomix® high-temperature recipes, you must use the given ingredient quantities for guaranteed success. The new high temperature heating offers an enhanced Thermomix® cooking experience; developing richer flavours and enabling new cooking techniques.

START COOKING

Always remember to insert the measuring cup, unless mentioned otherwise in a recipe.

Use the search function to find a recipe by name or ingredient, or find your selected recipes under **"My Week"**.

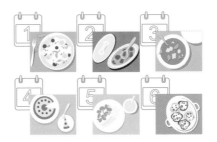

Select a recipe and view it from beginning to end by scrolling down. This is the same as reading the recipe from the cookbook but on a digital display.

You'll see clear, step-by-step instructions so you know exactly what you have to do. Time and temperature are preset so all you need to do is add the ingredients – Thermomix® will weigh them for you – and turn the speed selector.

Once you've completed a step, touch **"Next"** to see the following set of instructions.

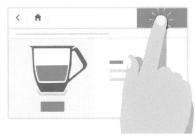

If you're more comfortable cooking manually, you can override Guided Cooking and adjust the settings to your own needs. Whether it's substituting ingredients or changing the cooking times, the decision is yours.

Good to know

Use the **splash guard** with high-temperature recipes to avoid hot splashes. Use the **simmering basket** or **Varoma dish** to allow steam to escape by placing on mixing bowl lid. These can also be used as sieves or colanders.

"With aid of spatula": when this is mentioned in a recipe, insert the Thermomix® spatula through the hole in the mixing bowl lid and rotate it to support mixing and chopping. No other utensil should be used in this way.

Use the **spatula** to remove the hot simmering basket as well as to scrape food out of the mixing bowl. The tip of the spatula is shaped to fit around the mixing knife, making it easier to remove any remaining ingredients.

Dislodging ingredients: after emptying the mixing bowl, a few seconds on speed 10 will project residues onto the sides of the mixing bowl, making them easy to remove with the spatula.

To weigh ingredients outside the mixing bowl, tare the scales and place the ingredients on the mixing bowl lid. Alternatively, place a container on the mixing bowl lid, tare the scales, then weigh ingredients into the container. You can also weigh ingredients on the mixing bowl lid while Thermomix® is active at low speeds.

Add ingredients to the simmering basket and Varoma **according to their cooking times,** placing faster-cooking ingredients (e.g. fish) on the Varoma tray. When placing ingredients in the Varoma, leave some holes unobstructed to ensure steam can circulate.

Cooking Your Own Recipes

Has there ever been a dish you were certain you could never make? An impressive dessert, a complex sauce, or a family-favourite yeasted loaf? Well now you can – with Thermomix®, everything is possible.

Whether it's a stew passed down from your grandparents, or a stylish new cake that's trending on social media, you'll likely have recipes of your own that you'd like to cook. With Thermomix®, these recipes will be easier than ever before. Once you've mastered the combination of time, temperature and speed, converting these recipes will be simple. Meanwhile, practice with tested Thermomix® recipes and understand how to "think" in the Thermomix® way.

Follow our tips and start creating and adapting your own recipes.

REFER TO A SIMILAR THERMOMIX® RECIPE

Before attempting to adapt your own recipes, first, familiarise yourself with Thermomix® by cooking some recipes from Cookidoo®.

Once you feel comfortable cooking with Thermomix®, search Cookidoo® for a recipe that has a similar method to the one you want to cook. Use the Thermomix® recipe as a template.

If the quantities of ingredients are significantly different, adjust cooking times. Make sure you don't exceed the capacity of the mixing bowl (max. 2.2 litres).

Adapt the method of the Thermomix® recipe to the needs of your recipe. Sometimes two steps in a traditional recipe can be achieved in a single Thermomix® step.

Finally, make your recipe with Thermomix®. Make notes on what works and what can be improved the next time you make it.

- **Cook or stew** at 90-100°C to retain as many nutrients as possible. Cooking time depends on ingredients, so refer to a similar Thermomix® recipe for guidance. Use ⟳ to stir or mix without chopping.

- **Cook with milk or cream** at 90°C to avoid overboiling. Stir sauces quickly to avoid lumps, on speed 2-4.

- **Cook/steam in the simmering basket or Varoma** ingredients such as vegetables, rice, prawns and meatballs. Add liquid to the mixing bowl, or cook them at the same time as you cook another dish in the mixing bowl.

Reorganise the steps in your recipes to minimise effort e.g. cleaning the mixing bowl. For example:

- **Dry to wet:** start with tasks that require a clean and dry mixing bowl (e.g. grinding sugar, chopping herbs).
- **Cold to hot:** knead dough, whip cream, blend drinks or chop onions before cooking sauces or soups.
- **All-in-one:** often several ingredients can be added at the same time, shortening a recipe.

Also, whenever possible, cook several dishes at the same time using the simmering basket and/or Varoma.

TIPS

- Make **grinding** grains, nuts or sugar and grating cheese or bread the first step. These tasks work best in a clean and dry mixing bowl and little to no cleaning will be required before the next step (see Resources p. 223).

- **Knead** bread, pizza or pasta dough before other tasks. These doughs are usually easy to remove from the bowl, which avoids unnecessary cleaning.

- **Mix** sauces, cake batters, pancake batters or biscuit doughs in a few seconds on speeds 2-5. Note that all ingredients can usually be mixed at once.

- **Whisking** egg whites requires a perfectly clean bowl, so start with this task whenever possible and remember to use the butterfly whisk at a maximum speed 4.

- **Chop** vegetables before sautéing them. Chopping vegetables together with oil can make it easier or sometimes even unnecessary to scrape down the mixing bowl between functions.

- **Sauté** onions or other chopped vegetables at 120°C for maximum flavour, for 3-7 minutes, depending on the ingredients' water content. Stir on speed ◁ to 1.

Don't forget to share photos of your family recipes and your own creations with us on Instagram and Facebook by tagging **@thermomixuk**

- ⓕ ThermomixUK
  ThermomixIrelandOfficial
- ⓘ @thermomixuk
- ⓣ @UKThermomix
  @ThermomixIre
- ▶ Vorwerk Thermomix UK

A Guide for Your Thermomix® Journey

Depending on your mood and schedule, you may feel like cooking in different ways. Creative or time-conscious, healthy or indulgent, organised or impulsive – Thermomix® can help you cook what you want, how you want it.

CHAPTERS
What do you need?

The chapters in this book are organised according to your needs. If you're looking for quick and easy recipes for daily meals, refer to the **Everyday Cooking** chapter. If you have more time and prefer to cook in advance, or if you're entertaining for a group of friends, have a look at the **Weekend Time** chapter. **Basics and Homemade** will enable you to stock your fridge and pantry with homemade staples so that every time you reach for a prepared ingredient, you know exactly what's in it. Finally, there's a **Special Occasions** chapter for those times when you want to really impress.

TIPS AND MASTERCLASSES
Learn more

In each chapter, you'll find editorials and masterclasses to support you on your Thermomix® journey. If you're a beginner, the masterclasses will help get you started, while more advanced cooks will find out how to put Thermomix® to work to create their own recipes. In every chapter, a selection of recipes illustrates the benefits described in the editorials.

RECIPES
Just a glimpse

Recipes are presented in a short version, with photos and main features, and enough information to let you choose what to cook. The complete recipes can be read on the screen of your Thermomix® in a digital version, from Cookidoo®. Before you start to cook, you can check the nutritional values and ingredients directly on your Thermomix®. We continuously update and improve our recipes and these improvements are delivered seamlessly to your kitchen via Cookidoo®.

Important
Please refer to the instruction manual and the safety notes on the device.

FROZEN FRUIT SORBET

A refreshing end to any meal, Thermomix® makes light work of preparing sorbets. Try our *Lemon* or *Papaya Sorbets*, or add a splash of alcohol to make *Champagne Grapefruit Sorbet*.

Special diets and food intolerances

- **Ovo-lacto vegetarian:** contains no meat or fish products, but eggs and dairy may be included.
- **Vegan:** contains no animal products.
- **Gluten free:** contains no gluten.
- **Dairy free:** contains no dairy products.

The short description gives you an insight into the recipe. Full details can be found on Cookidoo®.

Key information

- **Active time:** the hands-on time needed to prepare the recipe.
- **Total time:** the total time needed to prepare the dish from start to finish. Total time also includes baking times, cooling times, etc.
- **Servings:** how many portions or pieces the recipe makes.
- **Difficulty:** Easy, Medium, Advanced. You should be able to master all the recipes without any problems.

Some of them are more challenging than others and may require more of your time if you are new to cooking.

- **Nutritional values:** in this book we list only energy. You will find more detailed nutritional values in the recipe itself on your Thermomix®.
- **Essentials:** the key ingredients or useful items that are essential to the recipe's success.

5 min · 5 min

4 portions

Easy

Per portion: 133 kcal

Mixed frozen fruit, sugar

BE LA

Layer simple stoppi *Triple* and ev

30 m

12 s

Med

Per s

Eggs fres baki

Basics and Homemade

Store-cupboard ingredients: storing dried ingredients, such as pulses, rice, flour and sugar, in glass jars and bottles on exposed shelving creates an attractive focal point, and makes everything easier to find. Buy glass storage jars or collect a range of glass jars from finished preserve containers.

The Art of Storage

Well-organised shelves and attractive, functional storage solutions are good starting points for successful cooking. Experimenting with new recipes and cooking for family and friends is easier when utensils and ingredients are readily to hand.

Vegetables and produce storage: store in a cool, dark place where air can circulate. Place an apple with potatoes to stop them sprouting. Bamboo steamers are an attractive and practical way to store produce.

Fresh fruit and vegetables: refrigerate herbs in jars with their stems in water, covering the tops with a loose plastic bag. Spritz salad leaves and fresh vegetables with cold water and refrigerate in bags. Keep ripe tomatoes and other soft fruit in the fridge, only rinsing when ready to eat.

The Art of Cold Storage: storing foods properly in the fridge will keep them fresh longer, and avoid cross-contamination

Upper shelves

- Foods that need to be kept at a cool temperature, and/or will be eaten soon.
- Ready-to-eat prepared sauces, preserves, mayonnaise, pickles and fruit.

Middle shelves

- Foods to be stored at a cold temperature.
- Leftovers, cheese, cream, cooked and wrapped meats.

Bottom shelves

- Raw meat and poultry, fish, dairy products.
- NB: Store raw meat and poultry in a covered container to prevent juices leaking.

Vegetable and salad drawers

- The high humidity keeps vegetables and salads fresh. Keep in sealed bags or containers.

Door shelves

- Upper: condiments and vinaigrettes.
- Lower: all beverages.

TIPS

- Whole spices will last longer than ground spices. Grind whole spices in batches as needed, to preserve freshness.
- When kitchen space is limited, lay small jars or spices in shallow drawers with labels on the front. In deep drawers, stand the jars up, with labels on the lid.

Tins, jars and packets: if your cupboards are deep, use a turntable or multi-level shelving for tins and jars.

TIP | Clear labels are key to efficient storage. Write directly on the jar with an all-surface pen, buy labels to stick on, or make your own from coloured card and string, as pictured.

TIPS

- For fresh herbs and an attractive windowsill, grow in jars or pots.
- Store bananas and avocados at room temperature, separately from other produce. Once avocados have fully ripened, store in the fridge.
- Store apples in a cool, dark place separated by tissue or baking paper.

Meat and fish: avoid waste by freezing in portioned, clearly labelled freezer bags. Defrost as needed.

Cheese: grate in Thermomix® and freeze in bags, ready to use.

Bread: to make bread last, store wrapped in paper, in a bread bin if possible. Refrigeration will dry out bread and make it go stale quickly.

Nuts and spices: save time by organising spices in alphabetical order. Store spices in their whole form, clearly labelled, to make an attractive display. To avoid nuts turning rancid, you can freeze them, either whole or chopped.

Streamlining Your Cooking

Thermomix® takes care of kitchen tasks such as weighing, chopping and cooking, with recipes appearing on screen in front of you. This frees up space on your kitchen shelves and in your cupboards for the few basic utensils you need to create show-stopping dishes!

Place your Thermomix® in a suitable and convenient spot in your kitchen, ideally with no cupboards above to allow for easy steaming with the Varoma. Having it on a countertop with room either side ensures you have enough space for preparation and serving.

USING WHOLE AND FRESH INGREDIENTS

Keep some ingredients in their whole form – Thermomix® can chop and grind them as and when needed. For instance, just keep granulated sugar in your cupboard then grind into caster sugar or icing sugar as needed. Keep spices fresher for longer by buying in their whole form and grinding as needed. Flours are easy to make from whole grains and coffee can be ground from coffee beans. Follow the instructions in the Resources section on p. 223 to make your own ground ingredients with no additives.

TIP | The built-in scales will measure both liquids and solids. You can also place any bowl on top of the mixing bowl lid to weigh ingredients, meaning you never need another set of scales. Simply tare the scales to set it to zero and add your ingredient. You can even do this while Thermomix® is

ESSENTIAL UTENSILS

Here is your toolkit checklist - all you need to have to hand to assist your Thermomix® cooking, with a few optional extras.

Loaf tin

Tea towels

Casserole dish that can go straight to the table

Rolling pin

Chopping board

Non-stick frying pan

Cake tin

Pastry cutters

Vegetable peeler

Ramekins

Bowls in a variety of sizes

Tart tin

Baking tray

Kitchen string

Baking paper

Cling film

Aluminium foil

Wire rack

Kitchen scissors

operating at low speeds – allowing you to get your ingredients ready for the next step of your recipe.

CHOOSING A KNIFE

When you own a Thermomix®, you only need a small selection of quality knives to support your food preparation. The best knives are made with carbon steel as they have sharper edges. Look for ones with a comfortable handle for effortless chopping.

A paring knife is good for peeling or trimming vegetables and is useful for delicate work. A utility knife and a chef's knife can be used for slicing and chopping many different foods, as well as skinning and filleting fish. A larger carving knife is useful for large joints of meat, while a serrated knife is the best option for slicing bread. Regularly sharpening your knives will help make your cooking preparation easy.

Chef's knife

Utility knife

Paring knife

CHOOSING DISHES TO USE IN THE VAROMA

- Use heat-resistant materials such as ceramic, metal or silicone. Only use glass or plastic if you know it is heat-resistant (this is usually marked on the packaging).
- Before starting your recipe, place an empty dish in the Varoma and check the lid closes fully.
- Make sure a few holes in the Varoma dish and Varoma tray remain unobstructed so steam can circulate.

TIPS

- When you pack your Thermomix® up to take on holiday, be sure to set it to Transportation mode in the Settings menu.
- Even away from home, cooking with your Thermomix® is easy. Together with a sharp knife, large bowl and clean tea towel, you'll have everything you need to enjoy delicious, home-cooked food wherever you are.

Homemade Pantry

Stocking your pantry with everyday items made with your own ingredients is healthier, saves money, and reduces unnecessary packaging. With Thermomix® and a few basic ingredients, its easy to stock your entire pantry, fridge and freezer.

STORING AND PRESERVING

By observing good hygiene and best food practice, together with following the recipe precisely and preparing storage containers as directed, you can be assured that the foods you make can be stored for months to come.

In addition, making your own pantry items and preserving homemade goods helps reduce food and packaging waste, helping you play your part in looking after the environment.

Cleaning jars for longer storage life

The jars you use should be as clean as possible to extend the storage life of the preserves and pantry items, and stop any spoilage from bacteria.

How to prepare your jars for filling:
- Place 500 g water in the mixing bowl. Place jars and lids upside down in the centre of the Varoma and steam **20 min/Varoma/speed 1**. Leave to drain – do not dry or touch the inside surfaces. OR
- Thoroughly wash jars and lids in hot, soapy water. Rinse by pouring over boiling water. Prepare for filling, if needed, by placing on a clean tea towel in a roasting tin and heat in the oven at 100°C until required.

RECIPES FOR YOUR HOMEMADE PANTRY

Stock your shelves with homemade items for your family and friends. For instance, Thermomix® makes it easy to make your own **granola**...

... **cookies**...

... and **vanilla sugar** or **cinnamon sugar**, perfect for cakes or other sweet bakes.

Non-dairy milks are also easy to make with Thermomix®.

Make pesto from fresh ingredients quickly and easily in your Thermomix® then store in the fridge for up to one week. Instead of buying ready-made sauces and dips, choose a recipe from Cookidoo® and make your own at home.

TIP | Liven up lunches with a batch of zingy homemade *Barbecue Sauce*, then label and store the remainder in jars until needed.

HOMEMADE STOCK PASTES

There are no hidden ingredients when you make your own stock pastes. They're an excellent way to add flavour to any dish and, in sealed jars, will store for weeks in the fridge. Thermomix® recipes for *Vegetable Stock Paste*, *Chicken Stock Paste* and *Meat Stock Paste* can all be found on your Thermomix®.

TIPS

• White or brown distilled vinegar works effectively as a preserving agent, with white vinegar preserving the colour in vegetables better.
• You don't need to use special sugar for preserving; granulated is fine.

Start small with your pantry. Begin by choosing one or two items to make at home each week. Add to your weekly shopping list, and soon you'll have a pantry brimming with homemade goods.

STRAWBERRY JAM

With temperature-controlled cooking, making jam is easy with Thermomix®. A great way to use up an abundance of fruit when it is in season, refer to Cookidoo® for a range of preserve recipes.

🔪 15 min 🕐 55 min

🍲 Total recipe (approx. 800 g)

🌡 Easy

📊 Total recipe: 1704 kcal

🔑 Strawberries, sugar; glass jars with screw-top lids

CRUNCHY GRANOLA 🌿

Making homemade cereals and granolas means you can be confident of exactly what ingredients have gone into your breakfast. For more ideas to kick-start your day, search for breakfast bowls on Cookidoo®.

📐 1 h ⏲ 2 h

🍽 50 portions (approx. 40 g servings)

👨‍🍳 Medium

📊 Per portion: 167 kcal

🔑 Oats, seeds, nuts, dried fruit; baking trays, baking paper, airtight containers

BANANA AND OATMEAL ENERGY BARS

This healthier energy bar uses dates and bananas for natural sweetness. Combined with nutrient-rich oats, this is a simple recipe to prepare in your Thermomix®. Can also be made ahead and stored in airtight containers.

 10 min   1 h 10 min

 10 pieces

 Easy

 Per piece: 168 kcal

 Bananas, dates, walnuts, oats; square baking tin, baking paper, airtight container

SERIOUSLY SEEDY CRACKERS

An all-in-one dough recipe laden with nutritious seeds, this is an easy and cost-friendly recipe to have in your repertoire. Make and roll out the dough ahead of time, then leave in the fridge until ready to bake.

✎ 10 min ⏱ 30 min

🍞 35 pieces

👨‍🍳 Easy

📊 Per piece: 53 kcal

🔑 Seeds, bread flour; baking trays, baking paper, rolling pin, pastry cutter

Yoghurt

There is a huge variety of yoghurts available, all with different textures and flavours. With Thermomix®, you can create a version exactly how you like it – choose the amount of sugar you'd like or whether the yoghurt is thick or runny, depending on your taste. Different types of milk can also be used allowing you to cater for those following particular diets. Healthier and less expensive... follow these simple tips to make your own yoghurt at home.

TYPES OF YOGHURT

Yoghurt is simply fermented milk. Fermentation occurs when bacteria transform the sugar of the milk (lactose) into lactic acid. This happens when the milk is kept at a certain temperature for the right length of time.

TEXTURE
• **Set Yoghurt:** this is the most common type of yoghurt. It can be made by fermenting in the mixing bowl, or in individual yoghurt jars in the Varoma.
• **Greek-style Yoghurt:** this is a concentrated version of plain yoghurt, which has been sieved to become thicker. This recipe requires more milk for the same final volume of yoghurt, which is why shop-bought Greek yoghurt is often more expensive.

TIP | Make your own Greek yoghurt. Start by preparing plain yoghurt in the mixing bowl. Line the simmering basket with a muslin cloth or cheesecloth, set it over a bowl and spoon in the prepared yoghurt. Cover, refrigerate and allow to drain for 2-3 hours. The longer you leave it to drain, the thicker the result. Transfer your Greek-style yoghurt to yoghurt pots or airtight jars and serve or store in fridge.

• **Drinking Yoghurt:** this is a popular and convenient way to enjoy yoghurt, as a quick, grab-and-go snack. To make, simply mix your set yoghurt for a further **10 sec/speed 4**, then pour into bottles and store in the fridge until needed.

5 REASONS TO MAKE YOUR OWN YOGHURT

1. EASY TO MAKE
Only 10 minutes of hands-on time for you, then Thermomix® will maintain the optimum temperature for delicious yoghurt every time.

2. HEALTHIER
When you make homemade yoghurt, you know exactly what goes into it – there are no artificial flavours, colours, preservatives or stabilisers.

3. FOR ALL TASTES
Adjust the amount of sugar, the flavour and the texture, according to your taste – you can choose.

4. GOOD FOR THE ENVIRONMENT
Reduce waste by reusing yoghurt pots or jars.

5. SAVES MONEY
1000 g of milk is much cheaper than 1000 g of plain yoghurt. If you do the sums, you'll see how much you can save per year.

FLAVOURING
- **Plain Yoghurt:** nothing else is added apart from the yoghurt cultures.
- **Sweetened Yoghurt:** add sugar or another sweetener, such as honey or golden syrup.

TIP | For sweetened yoghurt, add 40 g sugar per 1000 g milk along with any other flavourings, before starting the fermentation.

- **Flavoured Yoghurts:** yoghurts can be made with many different flavours; vanilla, caramel, chocolate and fruit all work well. Flavoured yoghurts are usually sweetened too, so by making your own, you can control the amount, according to taste.

TIPS
- **Vanilla Yoghurt:** for 1000 g milk, add 40 g sugar and 1 tsp vanilla extract, or the seeds from half a vanilla pod, at the start of the recipe.
- **Caramel Yoghurt:** add 50-70 g caramel sauce per 1000 g milk at the start of the recipe.
- **Fruit-flavoured Yoghurt:** add 50-70 g jam or dried fruit, such as dates or dried apricots, along with the milk and any other ingredients, before you start fermentation.
  – Fresh fruit may hinder fermentation so make sure you only mix it in just before serving, either chopped or blended.
  – For an attractive presentation, place 1 Tbsp fruit jam or cooked fruit in the bottom of each yoghurt pot then pour the yoghurt on top.

MAKING PLAIN YOGHURT IN POTS

PREPARATION

Thoroughly clean the mixing bowl, knife and lid as well as yoghurt pots or airtight jars, to ensure optimal healthy bacteria growth.

Place 8 heat-proof containers (120 ml each) in the centre of the Varoma dish.

INGREDIENTS

The only ingredients you need to prepare homemade yoghurt are pasteurised whole milk and some plain yoghurt. Whole milk is ideal because the higher fat content will give you a thicker, creamier yoghurt. However, other types of milk can also be used.

TIPS

- **If using raw milk:** heat **15 min/90°C/speed 2**, then leave to cool to room temperature before starting the recipe.
- **Extra thickness:** gelatine, agar agar or milk powder can be added for extra thickness, or you can follow the steps described above for Greek-style yoghurt. The heating and cooling process described for raw milk can also be used with pasteurised milk to produce a thicker consistency.
- **Creamy yoghurt:** replace 100-200 g milk with single cream.
- **Low-fat yoghurt:** low-fat milk can be used, but the consistency of the yoghurt will not be the same. For a thicker consistency, add 1-2 Tbsp gelatine, dissolved in a bowl with a little warm milk, before adding to the other ingredients.
- **Yoghurt starter culture:** you can replace the plain yoghurt with a yoghurt starter, available in health food shops or online (follow the instructions on the packet).

MIXTURE

Place all ingredients in the mixing bowl then, when the mixture is ready, pour into the yoghurt pots to start the fermentation in the Varoma dish.

FERMENTATION

Place water in the mixing bowl and place Varoma into position.
The yoghurt will take approximately 8 hours to ferment.

TIPS

- Keeping the yoghurt warm and undisturbed during fermentation is essential to achieving the right texture.
- The cooler the room temperature, the longer the yoghurt should be left to incubate. In very warm environments, 8-10 hours may be sufficient.
- The longer the fermentation time, the more acidic the yoghurt.

STORAGE

After fermentation, refrigerate the yoghurt for at least 3 hours before serving.

IMPORTANT | Yoghurt can be stored in the fridge for a few days. If the sourness increases or you see signs of mould, the yoghurt has expired and you should discard it.

TIP | Remember to reserve some plain yoghurt as a starting culture for your next batch.

TM6
exclusive

PLAIN YOGHURT

Plain, unflavoured yoghurt is delicious on its own, or combine with other ingredients for an endless variety of flavours. Serve with fruit and cereal, or use in smoothies or ice creams. Yoghurt also works well in savoury dishes, providing a good base for dips, sauces or salad dressings.

- 10 min
- Approx. 12 h
- 8 portions
- Easy
- Per portion: 96 kcal
- Whole milk, plain yoghurt; 8 glass yoghurt jars

ALMOND MILK

Thanks to Thermomix® it's easier than ever to make your own nut milks. The powerful blending results in richly flavoured milk, in this case almond, although the method works equally well for other nut varieties.

🔪 10 min

⏱ 6 h 10 min (including soaking time)

🍞 Total recipe (approx. 1 l)

👨‍🍳 Easy

📊 Total recipe: 611 kcal

🔑 Almonds; muslin or nut milk bag, glass bottle

LEMON CURD

Fruit curds are so impressive with Thermomix®.
This lemon version is rich, zesty and full of flavour
and, with temperature-controlled heating,
perfect results are guaranteed every time. Serve
on toast or scones, or as a filling for cakes and
tarts. For other fruit varieties, try *Gooseberry Curd*
or *Seville Orange Curd*.

10 min 1 h

Total recipe (approx. 680 g)

Easy

Total recipe: 2135 kcal

Sugar, lemons, butter,
eggs; glass jars with
screw-top lids

CHOCOLATE HAZELNUT SPREAD

A rich and indulgent family favourite, this homemade version means you know exactly what it contains. Made using milk or dark chocolate, the capability of Thermomix® means you are heating and blending all in the same bowl.

10 min   45 min

Total recipe (approx. 450 g)

Easy

Total recipe: 2201 kcal

Chocolate, milk, hazelnuts, sugar; baking tray, glass jar with airtight lid

BASIL PESTO ⊗

Fresh, full of flavour, and ready in under 10 minutes, you'll never need to buy shop-bought again. Serve with pasta, use to fill chicken breasts or add flavour to fish fillets, then store the remainder in the fridge for up to 1 week.

- 10 min ⏱ 10 min
- Total recipe (approx. 350 g)
- Easy
- Total recipe: 1848 kcal
- Parmesan, pine nuts, basil, oil; glass jar with airtight lid

CARAMEL SAUCE

Flavour cookies, cakes and icings, stir into brownie batter, add to hot chocolate, or simply drizzle over ice cream. Always popular and so versatile, this sauce can be made up to 3 days ahead and kept in the fridge.

TM6 *exclusive*

🔪 5 min ⏱ 1 h 30 min

🍲 Total recipe (approx. 400 g)

👨‍🍳 Easy

📊 Total recipe: 2040 kcal

🔑 Sugar, cream, butter; glass jar with airtight lid

CARAMELISED RED ONION CHUTNEY

The high temperatures of Thermomix® caramelise the red onions for a fuller flavour in this tasty chutney. Serve with goat's cheese on crackers or crostini for a great canapé, or add to a cheese board.

✍ 10 min   ⏱ 1 d

🍲 Total recipe (approx. 400 g)

👨‍🍳 Easy

📊 Total recipe: 1215 kcal

🔑 Red onions, sugar, vinegar, olive oil; glass jar with airtight lid

Pastry

Mastering shortcrust pastry is easy with Thermomix®!
We'll take you through the entire process, including shaping
and decorating. Get ready to impress your friends and family
with freshly-baked tarts and pies!

INGREDIENTS AND UTENSILS

PLAIN FLOUR

A plain white wheat flour milled from
soft wheat varieties is best for making
pastry. It is lower in gluten and
protein than bread flour, meaning it
will shrink less. Wholemeal flour can
also be used, although it will result in
a denser pastry.

....

TIP | Replace 30 g of plain white flour
in your pastry recipe with wholemeal
flour or ground nuts for extra texture
and flavour.

SALT

In addition to providing flavour, salt
helps to brown the pastry and form a
golden crust.

BUTTER

For most shortcrust pastries, unsalted
butter is the best fat to use. It must be
as cold as possible so that it does not
melt, which would result in a greasy
pastry that is difficult to roll out.

....

TIP | If you don't want to use butter,
you can use cold coconut oil, cold
lard or cold olive oil. These will give a
different texture and flavour to the
finished pastry.

WATER

Water must be chilled to prevent the
pastry dough from warming up and
becoming greasy. You don't need to
use mineral water; tap water is fine.
The amount of water used may vary
slightly from the recipe, depending on
the absorbency of the flour and the
humidity of the kitchen. Use as little
liquid as possible to bind the pastry to
limit the amount of shrinkage during
baking.

OTHER INGREDIENTS

Egg, milk, icing sugar and flavourings
can also be added for a richer or
sweeter pastry.

USEFUL ITEMS

Equip your kitchen with some basic items to make your pastry baking a success. Baking paper, a rolling pin, baking beans or baking weights, a pastry brush for glazing, a metal tart tin and a wire rack are all essential. For crisper bases, bake on a flat, rimless baking sheet. The air will circulate around the base and the pastry will form a crust quicker.

STORAGE

Shape pastry dough into a flat disc and wrap in cling film, then store in the fridge for up to 3 days or in the freezer for up to 1 month.

TIP | To make it easier to defrost, roll out fresh pastry and place between sheets of baking paper (see tips for rolling out). Roll up into a log with the paper, and refrigerate or freeze.

Different Pastries

Shortcrust Pastry: this is the go-to pastry for many recipes, sweet or savoury. It is crisp and easy to make, with a firm texture that can be easily handled and shaped.

Sweet Shortcrust Pastry: icing sugar is added to give a sweet, crisp, golden-brown finish. It can be used for sweet tarts as well as for biscuits.

Puff Pastry: this is a rich, flaky pastry in which a large amount of butter is rolled between layers of dough. The dough is then folded over and rolled again, multiple times.

Quick Puff Pastry: butter is frozen in small cubes and mixed into the flour. The dough is then given a few folds as it is with traditional puff pastry.

MAKING SHORTCRUST PASTRY

THE PASTRY DOUGH

Mix only until the pastry starts to clump, then finish by bringing it together into a ball by hand. Over-mixed pastry becomes tough and difficult to shape. Wrap in cling film and refrigerate for 20 minutes. This resting period allows the gluten to relax, making the dough softer and easier to roll out.

TIPS | FOR SAVOURY PIES

• **Tomato Pastry:** replace the liquid with tomato purée.
• **Garlic and Coriander Pastry:** place 3 garlic cloves and 10 g coriander leaves in the mixing bowl then chop **8 sec/speed 3**. Add the ingredients for the shortcrust recipe and continue with step 1 of the recipe.
• **Basil and Lemon Pastry:** place zest of ½ lemon and 15 fresh basil leaves in the mixing bowl then chop **8 sec/speed 3**. Add the ingredients for the shortcrust recipe and continue with step 1 of the recipe. This is a great base for a tomato and mozzarella tart.

ROLLING OUT

To line a tart or pie tin, unwrap the dough, saving the wrapper to store any remaining dough. Sprinkle the surface and the rolling pin with a little flour. Roll out the dough in one direction, using light and even pressure on both ends of the rolling pin. Rotate the pastry as you go to ensure an even thickness. Use more flour if necessary to stop the pastry from sticking. When the circle is large enough to line the tin, roll it loosely over the rolling pin and unroll over the tin.

TIPS | FOR ROLLING OUT

• You can also cut dough into strips and use these to line the tin, pressing them in with your fingers.
• For a rich pastry, roll out between sheets of baking paper.
• If the dough gets too warm, leave in the paper and refrigerate or freeze for 10 minutes, then try again.

CUTTING OUT SHAPES

For sharp edges, rolled out pastry must be cool. Use a floured pastry cutter to cut out shapes, then transfer to a baking tray using a palette knife. Refrigerate before baking.

SHAPING PASTRY

Use your fingers to press the pastry into a tart tin, and repair holes with leftover dough. Trim any excess dough with a knife. Pinch the dough around the top edge with your thumb and forefinger to seal. To crimp pastry, put your forefinger on one edge and pinch pastry around it with your other thumb and forefinger. Repeat all around edge, then go around one more time to ensure the pastry is even.

FINISHING

Glaze pastry with a beaten egg, milk or cream and refrigerate for 15 minutes while the oven is preheating. For a deep glaze, brush again before baking.

BAKING THE PASTRY

To blind bake, prick the base of the dough, when in the tin, in several places with a fork. Line the pastry case with baking paper and fill with baking beans (dried beans can also be used). Push them into the corners to stop the base lifting in the tin as the pastry warms and bakes. For crisp pastry, bake at a high temperature (200°C is recommended).

Some ovens are hotter than others so you may need to make slight adjustments – the back and top of the oven are usually the hottest parts. An oven thermostat can be useful here.

COOLING

Pastry should be cooled quickly for a crisp finish, on a wire rack if possible. Alternatively, use a rack from the oven.

TIP | For a lighter pie top, instead of completely covering the pie in pastry, cut out pastry shapes and arrange over the top. This makes for less pastry as well as an eye-catching presentation, and works particularly well on smaller tarts.

SWEET SHORTCRUST PASTRY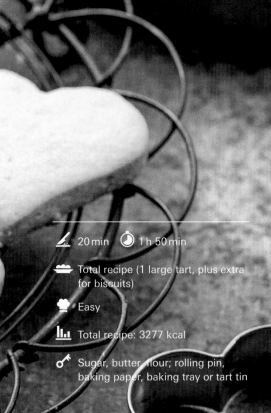

A crumbly pastry, enriched with egg, this is a
super simple and reliable Thermomix® recipe.
Use for sweet pie cases or to make biscuits.

✏ 20 min   ⏱ 1 h 50 min

🍽 Total recipe (1 large tart, plus extra
for biscuits)

👨‍🍳 Easy

📊 Total recipe: 3277 kcal

🔑 Sugar, butter, flour; rolling pin,
baking paper, baking tray or tart tin

QUICK PUFF PASTRY

This Thermomix® recipe simplifies a pastry that is traditionally more difficult to make. Chop frozen butter into flour in seconds, then create the layers by rolling and folding the pastry. It also freezes well – simply defrost in the fridge before baking.

🔪 20 min　⏱ 1 h 20 min

🍴 Total recipe (approx. 490 g)

👨‍🍳 Medium

📊 Total recipe: 2223 kcal

🔑 Butter, flour; rolling pin, baking paper, baking tray

PIZZA DOUGH

 5 min ⏱ 1 h

🍞 Total recipe (approx. 670 g)

🍴 Easy

📊 Total recipe: 1752 kcal

🔑 Bread flour, yeast, oil; large bowl, cling film

The Thermomix® kneading function makes light work of making dough. A simple recipe, requiring minimal effort on your part, spread the finished pizza dough with a homemade *Tomato Sauce* and toppings of your choice. For a gluten-free version, try the *Gluten-free Pizza* recipe on Cookidoo®.

BÉCHAMEL SAUCE

The most straightforward béchamel sauce recipe, this is one that you will return to time and time again, safe in the knowledge it will turn out perfectly every time, and without any effort!

- 10 min   15 min
- Total recipe (approx. 580 g)
- Easy
- Total recipe: 766 kcal
- Butter, flour, milk

BÉARNAISE SAUCE

This is a great sauce to serve with red meat. With your Thermomix® continually cooking, stirring and emulsifying, all at the same time, this sauce is quick and effortless.

⟋ 10 min   ⏱ 15 min

🍽 Total recipe (approx. 380 g)

👨‍🍳 Easy

📊 Total recipe: 1833 kcal

🔑 Shallots, wine, butter, egg yolks

CHOCOLATE SAUCE

Grate chocolate then melt to create this rich, velvety sauce. Try drizzling it over a bowl of ice cream, such as our classic *Vanilla Ice Cream* – look for the recipe on Cookidoo®.

 5 min 🕙 10 min

 18 portions

👨‍🍳 Easy

📊 Per portion: 257 kcal

🔑 Dark chocolate, butter, milk; glass jar with airtight lid

VANILLA CUSTARD ⊘ ⊗

For a thick, creamy vanilla custard, this reliable all-in-one recipe produces perfect results every time. For a thinner, pouring custard, use the *Crème Anglaise* recipe on Cookidoo®.

✎ 5 min ⏱ 15 min

🍲 4 portions

👨‍🍳 Easy

📊 Per portion: 192 kcal

🔑 Vanilla pod, milk, egg yolks, sugar, cornflour

FRUIT SAUCE (COULIS)

A fruit sauce that can be made with almost any in-season fruit, this is a great recipe to make the most of fruit when they are at their ripest. Served hot or cold, with sweet or savoury dishes such as roast meat, this is a very versatile recipe.

🔪 10 min ⏱ 10 min

🍱 Total recipe (approx. 320 g)

👨‍🍳 Easy

📊 Total recipe: 411 kcal

🔑 Fruit, sugar

Everyday Cooking

My Week

As well as being an extra pair of hands in the kitchen, Thermomix® is your assistant for all things meal planning. With Cookidoo®, you can create your weekly menu – browse recipes then add them to your calendar, amend with personal notes , then a shopping list will be automatically generated. When you're ready to cook, the recipes are at your fingertips. It's as easy as that!

THREE MAIN BENEFITS OF A WEEKLY MENU

EAT HEALTHIER

Meal planning can naturally lead to a more balanced diet. By deciding in advance what you are going to cook, you can make sure to include a variety of fresh, seasonal ingredients whilst also ensuring your diet includes a mix of meat, fish and vegetarian dishes. As well as being useful for evening meals, it also helps to plan for breakfasts, lunchboxes and snacks. Without a meal plan, it is easy to get into a rut of serving the same dishes and relying on ready-made foods and takeaways.

SAVE TIME

Cooking a larger quantity of food than needed and freezing the rest means you are preparing two meals at once. This ensures you can still enjoy a home-cooked meal on a busy day when cooking a meal from scratch would be difficult. In addition, using all four levels of the Thermomix® enables you to cook more than one dish at once (see Multi-level Cooking Masterclass p. 134).

SAVE MONEY

Writing a meal plan and a shopping list means you know the ingredients and quantities you need to buy, which avoids unneccessary waste. Planning makes impulse purchases easier to resist and cuts down on supermarket visits.

STEPS TO CREATE A WEEKLY MENU

CHECK YOUR WEEKLY SCHEDULE

Check your calendar for the week e.g. working late, childrens' activities, dinner out with friends, guests staying over, etc.

CHECK YOUR PANTRY

Before you make a weekly meal plan, check what ingredients you have in the pantry, fridge and freezer and make a note of what needs to be used first.

CHOOSE RECIPES

Select recipes based on total time, meal type, number of portions, dietary preference or occasion, and prepare your ingredients or dishes in advance (see the Get Ahead section on p. 142). With Cookidoo®, simply add the recipes to your calendar and they will be available in "My Week".

TIP | In-season ingredients typically taste better, and are fresher, more affordable, and at their nutritional best.

CREATE THE SHOPPING LIST

After making your plan, automatically generate a shopping list then edit if necessary. You are now ready to start your week.

TIPS

• **One step at a time**
If this is the first time you are creating a menu plan, start by planning for just two or three days, or only for dinners. Introduce the change gradually; once you have made a few weekly plans you may feel ready to start making a monthly menu.

• **Involve the family**
Encourage childen to pick out one or two meals for the weekly plan so that they feel more involved in the process. Creating a weekly menu can be a fun activity for the whole family.

• **Be creative**
With Cookidoo®, you have access to a wide variety of recipes from all around the world. Try introducing a new cuisine each week to broaden your culinary horizons, for example a vegetarian dinner, Chinese lunch or Mexican breakfast.

• **Reuse weekly plans**
Save time by re-using older weekly menus or including favourite recipes.

Setting aside just 30 minutes a week to create a meal plan could transform the way you and your family eat. If you have never used a meal plan before, you may find Thermomix® helps you make it a new habit.

PORRIDGE WITH FRESH FRUIT

Give yourself the best start to the day by enjoying a bowl of energy-rich porridge. In addition, this version is served with fresh fruit, so you'll be well on your way to five-a-day. For more delicious options, search for breakfast on Cookidoo®.

5 min   10 min

2 portions

Easy

Per portion: 387 kcal

Oats, oat milk, fruit

BIRCHER MUESLI

This continental recipe soaks oats overnight, making them easier to digest. Combined with raw fruit and topped with yoghurt, it makes a great alternative to processed, shop-bought cereals.

🔪 10 min ⏱ 8h 10 min

🍲 4 portions

👨‍🍳 Easy

📊 Per portion: 338 kcal

🔑 Apple juice, oats, nuts, dried fruit, desiccated coconut, yoghurt

SUNRISE SMOOTHIE

This fun, vibrant smoothie is made from scratch and packed full of goodness. Making smoothies fresh ensures maximum nutritional benefit. For more recipes, log on to Cookidoo® to see the huge range of possibilities.

- ⚒ 10 min
- ⏱ 10 min
- 🍽 7 glasses (150 ml each)
- 👨‍🍳 Easy
- 📊 Per glass: 113 kcal
- 🔑 Mango, pineapple, strawberries, bananas

ENERGISING SMOOTHIE

 5 min 🕐 5 min

🍴 2 glasses (300 ml each)

👨‍🍳 Easy

📊 Per glass: 510 kcal

🔑 Almond milk, bananas, oats,
peanut butter

This nutty banana smoothie contains energy-rich oats, making
it a great choice to kick-start the day. Thermomix® smoothies are
blended quickly and smoothly, resulting in nutrient-laden drinks
every time.

VEGETABLE AND HAZELNUT CHEESE MUFFINS

A great on-the-go lunch that can be adapted to include pancetta or ham. Whether you like savoury or sweet muffins, there are a whole variety of baking recipes for your Thermomix® available on Cookidoo®.

15 min   45 min

12 pieces

Easy

Per piece: 248 kcal

Cheese, carrots, hazelnuts, milk, flour, peas; paper muffin cases, muffin tin

SALMON AND COLESLAW SANDWICH FILLING

With Thermomix®, it's easy to whip up a creative, alternative lunch offering like this tasty sandwich filling. Enjoy on homemade *Baguettes* for the ultimate speedy midday meal.

✎ 10 min ⏱ 15 min

🥪 6 portions

👨‍🍳 Easy

📊 Per portion: 407 kcal

⚲ Oil, cabbage, carrots, smoked salmon, baguettes; jug

SPICED MOROCCAN LENTIL SOUP

Whether chunky or velvety smooth, all types of soup are possible in your Thermomix®. This spiced tomato version contains lentils, perfect for when you need an extra-filling lunch. Go online to find a huge variety of soups – there'll be something to suit every mood and season.

 10 min    40 min

4 portions

Easy

 Per portion: 236 kcal

Onions, lentils, spices, chopped tomatoes

SAVOURY FLAPJACKS

A savoury version of the well-known syrupy favourite, these flapjacks are a great way of getting children to eat more vegetables. Tasty cheese is combined with fresh herbs and vegetables to make an economical snack, or serve with a side salad for lunch.

5 min   45 min

12 pieces

Easy

Per piece: 152 kcal

Oats, vegetables, cheese, eggs; square baking tin, baking paper

CHICKPEA FLATBREAD AND CURRIED VEGETABLE DIP

Dips and breads are the perfect combination for a quick, healthy lunch, and both are so easy to make with a Thermomix®. Here, dried chickpeas are ground to make flour. Other flours can also be made thanks to the powerful motor and blade. Try with rice, quinoa, spelt or buckwheat.

15 min   50 min

4 portions

Easy

Per portion: 480 kcal

Chickpeas, aubergines, courgettes, chopped tomatoes, sesame seeds, spices; baking tray, baking paper

RICE SALAD WITH EGGS AND TUNA

A colourful and nutritious all-in-one meal to feed the whole family, rice is cooked in the simmering basket while eggs and vegetables are steamed in the Varoma above. Adapt the recipe to your tastes by using a different variety of rice, or try adding sweetcorn or mozzarella cheese before serving.

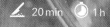 20 min · 1 h

 4 portions

Easy

Per portion: 485 kcal

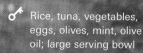 Rice, tuna, vegetables, eggs, olives, mint, olive oil; large serving bowl

BROCCOLI SALAD WITH RED PEPPERS AND PINE NUTS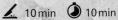

Thermomix® makes chopped salads in seconds. Here, raw, crunchy vegetables are chopped together with the dressing ingredients to create a fresh, colourful salad full of vitamins and minerals.

✎ 10 min ⏲ 10 min

🥘 6 portions

👨‍🍳 Easy

📊 Per portion: 107 kcal

🔑 Broccoli, red pepper, apple, pine nuts, olive oil, vinegar, honey, mustard

VERSATILE SMOOTH SOUP

 15 min   45 min

 6 portions

 Easy

 Per portion: 111 kcal

🔑 Mixed vegetables, vegetable stock

Try this smooth soup with your favourite ingredients to make it your own. Freeze soup in portions for easy defrosting and reheating later.

Risotto

While Italy is famous for pasta, there are also over one hundred varieties of rice grown and eaten there. Northern Italy has the ideal conditions for growing rice; flat lands and an abundance of water, which is why risotto is popular in the region. The main characteristics of a cooked risotto are the 'al dente' grains and a creamy texture. Traditionally, the cook stirs the rice constantly over an even heat, while adding hot stock. This constant stirring and attention to temperature produces a creamy sauce and perfectly-cooked rice. Thermomix® gradually stirs and cooks the risotto, saving you time, while guaranteeing delicious results every time.

RICE

Medium grain, 'semifino' rice varieties are used to make risotto. Carnaroli rice is the most widely used because it absorbs a lot of liquid while keeping its shape. Arborio and baldo are also popular varieties that hold their shape well while absorbing a large amount of liquid.

Rice contains no gluten which makes risotto a good option for those following a gluten-free diet. If risotto rice is unavailable, use another medium grain rice, or a short grain rice. A parboiled rice will not result in the creamy sauce, as the other varieties will. Use 80 g rice per portion for risotto.

TIP | Toasting the rice in oil or butter before adding liquid adds flavour and texture. Stirring the rice in the hot stock rubs the starchy outer layer and mixes it in with the stock, making the creamy risotto sauce. This is why the variety of rice is important when making a good risotto.

STOCK

Stock is the key component to a tasty risotto. Use chicken, beef, fish or vegetable stock according to your recipe, or, ideally, use homemade Thermomix® stock paste and boiling water for the best flavour. Always add hot stock to your risotto which, when making in Thermomix®, can be added all in one go; there is no need to stand over it stirring while adding the liquid gradually. Quick, easy and with no compromise on taste!

INGREDIENTS

PARMESAN CHEESE

Finely grate 10 g Parmesan cheese per portion in your Thermomix®, and fold into the risotto at the end, together with 10-15 g butter. The risotto is set aside to stand while the cheese and butter melt in, adding to the creaminess of the sauce. Grating Parmesan in Thermomix® couldn't be easier – remember to do it before you start cooking the risotto.

ONIONS

Chopped onions are cooked in oil and butter until translucent but without browning, because this would affect the flavour of the risotto. This is the soffritto, the first step of cooking the risotto.

OIL AND BUTTER

A mix of olive oil and butter is a good combination for flavour and texture, but oil alone can be used, according to personal preference. Rice is lightly toasted in oil or butter at the beginning of the recipe, the 'tostatura', without browning. At the end of the recipe, cold butter is carefully folded into the risotto and allowed to rest for 1 minute.

TIP | 'Mantecare' is the Italian word for the process of stirring in butter and Parmesan cheese to coat the rice and encourage the starch and fat to blend together. This creates a flavourful combination of rice, stock and cheese.

WINE

Dry white wine is stirred into the hot rice at the start of cooking then reduced to add a richness and acidity to the risotto. Use 15-20 g of wine per 80 g rice.

....

TIP | If you prefer, leave out the white wine and add in acidity in the form of 2 parts water and 1 part vinegar, to taste. Start with 5 g vinegar and 10 g water per portion.

SEASONING

Salt and freshly ground black pepper can be added at the end of cooking, according to your taste and preference.

RISOTTO TEXTURE

The finished risotto will be deliciously creamy and velvety, with the grains wet in the stock, but not swimming in it. The risotto should move as one, but not be too liquid like a soup or casserole, nor dry like a pudding. Italians call this texture 'all'onda', or 'wavy'; when the pan is shaken, a wave flows over the surface of the risotto.

RISOTTO EVERY DAY

Risotto is a dish that can only be appreciated when cooked and eaten straightaway; the uniquely creamy texture and the blended flavours are at their peak when just cooked. "Guests can wait for a risotto but risotto cannot wait for guests" is a well-known saying about this popular Italian dish. A Thermomix® risotto is an easy and quick option for every day. Choose your favourite recipe and in no time at all, you'll have a creamy, warming risotto to enjoy.

TIPS FOR SUCCESS

- Add extra butter at the end for a creamier texture.
- White wine can be left out or substituted with water and vinegar or stock, according to preference (see tip).
- Leave to rest for 1-2 minutes before serving.
- Add additional ingredients such as mushrooms, asparagus, red chicory or blue cheese at the end of cooking for extra flavour.
- Risotto is a very versatile base for a lot of flavourings. Try adding spinach to make a green risotto, or beetroot for a purple one.

RISOTTO WITH PARMESAN CHEESE

✎ 15 min

⏱ 30 min

🍴 4 portions

👨‍🍳 Easy

📊 Per portion: 433 kcal

🔑 Parmesan, butter, risotto rice, stock

Delicious Parmesan risotto is a great basic dish. Try adapting the flavour with these additions:
- **Saffron Risotto:** add 2 pinches saffron with the water.
- **Mushroom Risotto:** add 250 g fresh mushrooms (cut in pieces if too large) or 50 g dried mushrooms (soaked in water for 30 minutes, water squeezed out) with butter. Proceed as directed by recipe.
- **Tomato and Basil Risotto:** add 100 g chopped fresh tomatoes and 2 Tbsp fresh basil leaves along with butter.

Note that the maximum quantity of rice that can be cooked at any one time for this basic recipe is 500 g.
Keep in mind that adding other ingredients (e.g. mushrooms or sausage) will add volume to the dish, so adapt the rice quantity accordingly.

TIP | Leftover risotto can be transformed into patties known as 'arancini'. Cool the leftover risotto down quickly and store in the fridge for up to one day. When the rice is cool, make into patties, and stuff with a piece of mozzarella. Roll in breadcrumbs then fry until hot all the way through.

Making good risotto the traditional way takes time, attention and effort. Thermomix® will make authentic risotto for you, cooking at the perfect temperature and stirring at the right speed, for a perfect velvety risotto every time.

PASTA IN TOMATO SAUCE WITH CHORIZO

Pasta has long been a family favourite. Here the pasta is cooked in a homemade sauce in the mixing bowl, making this a great all-in-one dish that can be on the table in 20 minutes.

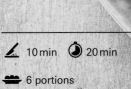

✎ 10 min   ⏱ 20 min

🍲 6 portions

👨‍🍳 Easy

📊 Per portion: 303 kcal

🔑 Tomato sauce, penne, chorizo, mushrooms

SPAGHETTI CARBONARA

 10 min ⏱ 35 min

 4 portions

 Easy

📊 Per portion: 604 kcal

⚙ Spaghetti, bacon cubes,
Parmesan, eggs; large serving
bowl

This popular dish full of rich cheese and salty bacon is so simple
to make when you use Thermomix®. The spaghetti disappears
through the hole in the mixing bowl lid as it softens and cooks.
For many more pasta recipes, visit Cookidoo®.

ORZO PASTA WITH SALMON AND SPINACH

A colourful and creative pasta dish that uses all the levels of Thermomix®. Omega 3-rich salmon is steamed in the Varoma above orzo pasta, cooked in stock to absorb flavours. Combined with spinach, cherry tomatoes and a creamy sauce, this is a great evening meal choice.

✎ 25 min ⏱ 40 min

🍽 4 portions

👨‍🍳 Easy

📊 Per portion: 560 kcal

🔑 Salmon, orzo, cream, spinach, cherry tomatoes

SEAFOOD RISOTTO

Risottos normally involve continuous stirring while adding hot stock one ladleful at a time. With Thermomix®, all the hard work is done for you, and the result will be a beautifully creamy dish that will impress anyone who tastes it.

✎ 20 min ⏱ 40 min

🍲 6 portions

👨‍🍳 Medium

📊 Per portion: 458 kcal

🔑 Mixed seafood, risotto rice, wine, stock, chopped tomatoes

TAGLIATELLE WITH PORCINI MUSHROOMS ⊘ ⊠

This recipe uses two types of mushrooms for greater depth of flavour. Dried pasta cooks beautifully in the mixing bowl, however, if you prefer, you can make your own *Pasta Dough* from scratch.

✎ 25 min ⏱ 1 h

🍽 4 portions

👨‍🍳 Easy

📊 Per portion: 396 kcal

🔑 Mushrooms, tagliatelle

ASIAN-STYLE CHICKEN, RICE AND VEGETABLES

A great all-in-one dish that the whole family will enjoy, chicken, vegetables, rice and sauce are all cooked perfectly in this simple dinner bursting with Asian-inspired flavours.

 15 min 40 min

4 portions

Easy

Per portion: 537 kcal

Chicken, onions, peppers, rice, broccoli, carrots; large serving bowl

Meat-free Main Course

Recent studies show that interest in reduced meat diets is rising due to health, environmental and sustainability concerns. Whether you'd like to reduce your meat consumption, increase the quantity of vegetables in your diet, or follow a vegetarian or vegan diet, Thermomix® can help you cook meat-free meals with confidence. Our masterclass will introduce meat-free options and tasty ideas that will satisfy everyone, whether vegetarian or not.

Vegetarian (vɛdʒɪˈtɛːrɪən)
Noun: a person who eliminates meat, fish, and sometimes other animal products from their diet.

Vegan (ˈviːg(ə)n)
Noun: a person who does not eat or use animal products.

BALANCED MEALS

In a reduced meat diet, a balanced plate, and well thought-out combinations of ingredients are important for good nutrition as well as a satisfying meal. Proteins from a variety of sources mean that all necessary amino acids are available. Use two or more sources of plant protein in one meal, for instance peas, beans, pulses, soy beans, soy-based products, nuts and seeds. Alongside this, serve a generous variety and amount of leafy vegetables and root vegetables together with carbohydrates such as whole grains, oats and wholewheat pasta to deliver a rich source of nutrients and fibre. This will add up to a balanced meal that will satisfy vegetarians and meat eaters alike.

TIP | If you decide to follow a vegan diet, it could be worth seeking advice to ensure you are consuming the right balance of nutrients, and consider including additional dietary supplements if needed.

SOY BEANS AND SOY PRODUCTS

Soy is an extremely versatile ingredient and a great source of protein, available in the form of soy beans, edamame beans or processed as tofu. Steamed whole edamame beans make a quick and simple appetiser: dip in soy sauce or sprinkle with coarse salt and eat the beans, discarding the pod.

Tofu is a popular choice for meat-free diets. Made from separating and pressing fresh soya milk, it provides a rich source of iron and calcium. It is also a versatile option; simply marinate then grill, bake or stir fry.

NUTS

Tasty and satisfying, nuts are great for meat-free diets. As well as being a good source of protein, nut oils are low in saturated fats including omega-3 fatty acids, thought to protect the heart. Add nuts to a curry, toss in a salad, blend and shape into a nut loaf, or soak and make into a 'cheese'. Alternatively, simply roast, toss in paprika and serve as a snack. With Thermomix®, it is easy to make nut milk by soaking and blending your choice of nuts, before draining and using the milk.

SEEDS

Linseeds, pumpkin seeds, chia seeds and sesame seeds are all good sources of protein and easy to use. Soak chia seeds overnight and stir into fruit for breakfast or cook up into a porridge with milk.

PULSES

Pulses are incredibly versatile and there is a huge variety available; soft, textured, quick cook or slow cook. Tinned pulses and beans are perfect for making a quick casserole, adding bold flavour and a portion of protein. For example, try adding tinned black beans to a beef casserole – this not only adds texture but is also an economical way to add bulk to a recipe and make a meal go further.

LEAFY GREENS AND VEGETABLES

Leafy greens and vegetables are packed with nutrients and are great for adding flavour, texture and colour to your dishes. Sauté or steam your vegetables in your Thermomix®, or simply chop to serve raw.

....

TIPS | USE IT ALL

• Once a week, clean and organise your fridge. Use up any remaining vegetables by making a puréed soup, vegetarian risotto, pizza, quiche or vegetable purée.

• Use whole vegetables to reduce waste. Vegetables such as courgettes, sweet potatoes, beetroot and squash can simply be washed and cooked.

• Save the vegetable scraps (skin, ends, tops and stalks) to make a stock. Stalks can also be used in soups.

MEAT-FREE MEALS

RICE BOWLS

Rice bowls, also called Buddha bowls, are hearty, filling and full of colour and texture. Place cooked whole grains, such as brown rice, in the base of the bowl then top with raw or cooked greens. Arrange avocados, legumes or vegetables, such as grated carrot or shredded cabbage, on top then finish with nuts, seeds or sprouts. Drizzle over your favourite dressing to finish. A rice bowl is a great way to try out new ingredients and vegetables in different flavour combinations.

BURGER IN A BUN

This is a popular meal: a toasted bun, salad dressing, coleslaw, mayonnaise, tomato ketchup, barbecue sauce and burger patty. All of these parts can be adapted for vegetarians or vegans. Thermomix® is the perfect tool to cook and blend pulses or soy beans and other healthy ingredients into a satisfying patty that ticks many of the flavour boxes of traditional meat burgers. Finish by making a homemade sauce, full of your favourite fresh ingredients. The buns can also be homemade; just toast then serve with a bean burger, coleslaw and salad greens accompanied by your choice of sauces and sides.

TAPAS/ MEZZE/ FEASTING

Creating a tapas-style meal, with several small plates of different foods around a theme, is easy with Thermomix®. Cook pasta or rice in the simmering basket and a sauce in the mixing bowl. Serve with a dressed salad, warm bread and vegan mayonnaise. Make a homemade guacamole to serve alongside and bring it all together.

QUINOA

Quinoa is a South American seed with red, black and white varieties. The white variety is the most widely used. Quinoa has a higher protein content than most grains, is gluten free and low in carbohydrates. Nutritionally, it is a good all-rounder, and a valuable source of plant protein.

COOKING QUINOA

Quinoa can be cooked in the simmering basket or directly in the mixing bowl. To cook quinoa in the simmering basket, simply follow the instructions for white rice in the appliance. Rinse before cooking.

Use the spatula to remove the hot simmering basket.

SERVING QUINOA

Serve quinoa plain or add chopped herbs to flavour. It is also delicious with chopped nuts or cooked peas stirred through.

Cold cooked quinoa is excellent as a salad base: try adding grated carrots, seeds, nuts and chopped apples for a tasty fruit and nut salad.

Try with cooked chopped beans, nuts and avocado combined with a houmous dressing for a great packed lunch. Stir some cooked quinoa into a burger patty mixture, or use to stuff vegetables such as tomatoes or aubergines.

This versatile ingredient is common in a meat-free diet. Try eating it in a variety of ways and mixed with different ingredients. Refer to Cookidoo® for a wide range of quinoa recipes.

STEAMED TOFU

The Varoma is great for steaming individual parcels
of delicate foods such as tofu, vegetables or fish.
A healthy and versatile way of cooking, you can
even steam desserts such as *Pineapple Parcels*!

 10 min 30 min

4 portions

Easy

Per portion: 332 kcal

 Tofu, mushrooms,
spinach, carrots, garlic,
soy sauce; baking paper

ROOT VEGETABLE HOTPOT WITH HARISSA

Thermomix® is ideal for one pot meals such as this healthy main which works well served with crusty bread. A great midweek meal choice to feed all the family, refer to Cookidoo® for more family meal inspiration.

 10 min 40 min

4 portions

Easy

Per portion: 185 kcal

Mixed root vegetables, haricot beans, harissa

MUSHROOM STROGANOFF

This is a tasty vegetarian alternative to the traditional meat-based dish. For many more ideas, such as *Vegetarian Chilli*, or *Lentil and Pumpkin Pot Pies*, refer to Cookidoo®.

🔪 10 min   ⏱ 30 min

🍽 4 portions

👨‍🍳 Easy

📊 Per portion: 218 kcal

🔑 Mushrooms, onions, double cream, wine

MEDITERRANEAN PEARL BARLEY RISOTTO

Thermomix® risottos are deliciously creamy and super easy to make. Traditionally made with rice, there are so many other grains that can be used. This one uses barley which is an excellent source of fibre giving a healthier twist to a classic dish.

🔥 15 min   ⏱ 1 h

🍽 4 portions

👨‍🍳 Medium

📊 Per portion: 517 kcal

🔑 Pearl barley, courgettes, wine, almond butter, sun-dried tomatoes; frying pan

COURGETTE, CORN AND RICOTTA PANCAKES ⊘

Thermomix® is great for whipping up quick pancake batters with healthy ingredients, such as this savoury version. For sweet options, look at *Walnut and Blueberry Bran Pancakes* or try *Apple Pancakes* for a delicious dessert.

📐 40 min   ⏲ 1 h 5 min

🍽 Total recipe (approx. 920 g)

👨‍🍳 Easy

📊 Total recipe: 273 kcal

🔑 Milk, courgettes, sweetcorn, flour, buttermilk, eggs, vinegar; muslin, large jug, frying pan, ladle, fish slice

STUFFED PEPPERS WITH HERBED QUINOA

 15 min   30 min

🍲 6 portions

👨‍🍳 Easy

📊 Per portion: 246 kcal

🔑 Quinoa, mixed peppers, vegetarian hard cheese, fresh herbs, olives, pine nuts

Stuffed vegetables make a great main course. The filling is made in the Thermomix® mixing bowl, then the stuffed peppers steamed in the Varoma. Also try *Tomatoes Stuffed with Mushrooms and Nuts*, or *Stuffed Butternut Squash with Feta*.

Fish and Seafood

Quick to cook, tasty and versatile, with numerous health benefits, fish is a popular choice for many. Fish contains many nutrients, including easy-to-digest proteins, omega-3 fatty acids, selenium, potassium and iodine, as well as vitamins A, B and D. This masterclass will show you how to confidently buy fish and seafood, use it in delicious recipes, and offer ideas of how to include more fish in your diet.

CUTS OF FISH

Here are some of the most popular cuts:

- **Whole** fish are easy to cook and are a more affordable option. They can be stuffed with different flavours and steamed or baked. Serve whole at the table.
- **Fish fillets** are boneless pieces of fish, usually in single portion sizes, making them easy to steam quickly. Tail end fillets are flatter, and fillets cut from the loin part are thicker.
- **Fish steaks** are pieces with the spine in. The large bones will hold the fish together and keep it more succulent as it cooks. Large fish, such as tuna and swordfish steaks, will be boneless.

SKINNING FISH

Some recipes call for skinless fish. This is the standard method for removing fish skin:

- Specialist fish knives have very thin blades and are very flexible, in order to cut the fillet cleanly. Alternatively, use the sharpest knife you have. Ensure the fish is chilled to make it easier to cut.

- Lay the fish skin-side down on a chopping board and hold the skin of the tail end, or the corner of the skin, with a clean tea towel to help you grip.

- Hold the knife firmly in your other hand, at right angles to the fish then, start cutting across the fillet, turning the blade away from you at a 45° angle to the fish skin so that the knife is cutting the fillet cleanly from the skin. Roll the fillet away from the skin as you cut.

- Push the blade of the knife along between the skin and the flesh, angling the blade towards the skin, and removing as much flesh as possible.

FISH TYPES AND COOKING

OILY FISH

Salmon, mackerel, trout, tuna and swordfish are oily fish that are bursting with flavour and packed with healthy omega-3 fatty acids. Very versatile, they can be steamed or baked whole, as well as served raw. Oily fish also make great fishcakes, patties and pâtés. Serve with lemon juice and black pepper, capers, tarragon or black olives.

TIP | Salmon en papillote is one of the simplest recipes. Place salmon fillet(s) on a sheet of baking paper, add extra ingredients such as cherry tomatoes, red onions or dill, fold and seal the paper. While steaming in the Varoma, the ingredients will flavour the fish. Check Cookidoo® for other recipes that are cooked 'en papillote' (in parcels).

WHITE FISH

Cod, haddock, pollock, ling, coley, plaice and sole are examples of white fish, delicately flavoured and easy to cook. These fish are best cooked quickly as fillets, steaks, or in pieces. White fish makes a tasty pie filling using a cooking method such as steaming or braising, or added to a casserole at the end of cooking in a béchamel sauce.

TIP | Sprinkle white fish fillets with salt before steaming in the Varoma; for a lemon flavour, arrange the fish fillets over a layer of lemon slices on the Varoma tray.

Buying Guide

Fresh fish has no smell, looks plump and appealing, and has firm flesh. Frozen fish is a great substitute as it is frozen when fresh which keeps nutrients intact. It's also really convenient as it can be stored in the freezer until needed. It can still be used in a recipe specifying 'fresh fish'; just defrost fully before cooking.

RIVER FISH

Perch, trout or zander (pike-perch)
are examples of this lean, white and
firm-fleshed fish. They have a subtle
flavour and are usually cooked in
fillets, fishcakes or patties.

TIP | Refrigerate leftover cooked fish
and store for up to 2 days. Peel
shellfish before storing. Fish tacos
are a great way to serve leftover
white fish, shellfish or oily fish. Simply
toss in a fajita seasoning then serve
in taco shells with salad and
guacamole. Make fish burgers from
cooked fish or seafood and mashed
potato, and serve with a tartar sauce.
Alternatively, try whipping into a
mousse or adding to a fish chowder.

SEAFOOD

Mussels, clams and scallops should
be kept in cold water after purchase.
To prepare, discard any that are open,
then scrub clean. Mussels have a few
hair-like strands on the shell – pull
these off and discard. Also discard
any shells that are not opened after
cooking. When steaming shellfish
in the Varoma, juices will go into the
cooking water and give it flavour.
Use between 300 g and 500 g water
for maximum flavour. Place the
Varoma containing the shellfish on
the mixing bowl lid only when Varoma
temperature has been reached and
the water is boiling. Cooked shellfish,
mussels and clams can be shelled and
the meat frozen for use in another dish.

TIP | Seafood is delicious with pasta.
Try these tasty combinations from
Cookidoo®: *Crab and Prawn Linguini
with Rocket, Pasta and Spicy Prawns
with Ginger*, or *Pasta with Prawns,
Courgette and Lemon*.

Prawns can be bought frozen or
fresh, raw or cooked, and in many
sizes. A Thermomix® recipe will
specify which kind is needed, but as
a broad guide, raw shell-on prawns
have the best flavour while the shell
also protects the prawns from the
heat of cooking. Small prawns are
just as tasty as larger ones, and
particularly convenient when
purchased cooked and frozen.
Mid-sized frozen prawns are the most
versatile and good to have in the
freezer. Prawns can be served hot in a
risotto, stir-fry or paella; or served
cold with mayonnaise or aioli.

COOKING METHODS

Peel and devein a prawn or shrimp
First remove the head and tail then, starting at the thickest end, move your thumb along the prawn, lifting the shell. You will find that halfway down the shell peels away easily.

Using a small knife, cut along the outer edge of the prawn's back, then remove and discard the vein.

Did you know...? This elegant starter of *Salmon Tartare* is quick to prepare in Thermomix®. It takes just 5 seconds to chop the fish along with all its flavouring ingredients.

Marinating: oily fish and seafood are best for marinating. Use oil and lemon juice as a base and season with garlic, herbs or other flavourings. Marinate for up to one hour before baking or steaming.

Steaming: all fish can be steamed in the Varoma. Line the Varoma tray first with baking paper if you want to collect the fish juices, then place any seasonings on the fish. The fish will cook quickly and the end result will be juicy and succulent.

Poaching: bring water to the boil before adding the simmering basket containing fish fillets or steaks. This is a delicious way to cook fish.

Casserole: prepare a light, flavourful fish casserole. First make your sauce, such as a curry sauce, a tomato and garlic sauce, or a simple parsley, lemon and garlic version. While the sauce is cooking, steam your fish in the Varoma, **10-15 min/Varoma/speed 1** then add to the sauce for a delicious casserole.

Raw: many kinds of fish are delicious raw. Ceviche is thinly sliced white fish that is marinated in a citrus juice liquor. Raw oily fish is delicious in sushi and sashimi, and also in *Salmon Tartare*.

To test if fish is cooked: check the thickest part. The flesh should be white and not translucent and it should flake easily with a fork.

PRAWN TACOS

These tacos, with a delicious sharp-but-sweet pineapple dressing, make a tasty, light evening meal that can be on the table in 30 minutes. Serve with salad and refried beans.

 5 min   30 min

12 pieces

Easy

Per piece: 143 kcal

Prawns, pineapple, taco shells

SALMON AND COUSCOUS PARCELS WITH SUN-DRIED TOMATOES

Steaming in paper parcels keeps all of the flavour in and is a healthier way of cooking as it doesn't require extra fats. The Varoma is the perfect accessory for all your steaming needs.

 15 min   35 min

 4 portions

Easy

Per portion: 460 kcal

Salmon, sun-dried tomatoes, couscous, herbs; baking paper

COD WITH OLIVE AND BREAD TOPPING, POTATOES AND TENDERSTEM BROCCOLI

This dish is a complete meal to feed all the family –
two vegetable sides complement the flavoursome
topped fish. To make *Cornbread* for
the topping, refer to Cookidoo®.

🍴 15 min　⏱ 40 min

🍽 6 portions

👨‍🍳 Easy

📊 Per portion: 307 kcal

🔑 Cod, cornbread, olives, cherry tomatoes,
new potatoes, tenderstem broccoli; baking
tray, baking paper, pastry brush, roasting tin

MUSSELS IN CREAM AND WHITE WINE SAUCE

 25 min   45 min

🍴 4 portions

👨‍🍳 Easy

📊 Per portion: 223 kcal

🔑 Mussels, onions, wine, double cream, garlic

Thermomix® is ideal for steaming shellfish and the Varoma can hold up to 1 kg mussels, perfect for this recipe. In addition, the juices from the mussels drip into the mixing bowl imparting more flavour into the sauce.

LEMON AND HERB SALMON BURGERS WITH PARMESAN COURGETTES

This is a great example of all the elements of a meal being made in your Thermomix®: the burgers, mayonnaise and courgette coating – you can even make the burger buns if you have time!

✎ 20 min   ⏱ 30 min

🍴 4 portions

👨‍🍳 Easy

📊 Per portion: 982 kcal

🔑 Salmon, courgettes, oil, peas, Parmesan; baking tray, baking paper, jug, frying pan

PAD THAI NOODLES WITH PRAWNS

Thermomix® is great for Asian food – whether steaming prawns and an omelette as part of this Pad Thai or cooking rice for *Coconut Rice with Asian-inspired Pork and Eggs*, the results are always fantastic and flavourful.

25 min   30 min

4 portions

Easy

Per portion: 352 kcal

Prawns, rice noodles, peanuts, bean sprouts, coriander; baking paper, large bowl

Meat and Poultry

Meat and poultry feature in many families' diets. This masterclass will show you how to buy and store fresh meat, which cuts to use, and easy techniques to help you with your daily cooking. We will demonstrate tips and techniques for cooking meat in your Thermomix®, to use alongside the thousands of recipes available on Cookidoo®.

TYPES OF MEAT

RED MEAT

Red meat, such as beef, pork or lamb, is available in different cuts. The back of the animal (e.g. loin, ribs, rump) is usually more tender than the front (e.g. legs, flank, shoulder).

Different meat cuts can be cooked in different ways. Tender cuts with more marbling from fat are best cooked faster and on higher temperatures. They are ideal for pan-frying, grilling or roasting.

Less tender cuts with more muscle tissue and less fat should be cooked longer and at lower temperatures. They tend to be good for slow cooking techniques such as baking, steaming or stewing. These cuts can also be marinated before cooking to tenderise and add flavour.

....

TIP | Use the high temperature settings of your Thermomix® to brown meat. Tender meat cut into strips can be browned, for example in a stroganoff. Less tender meat, cut into cubes, can also be browned, to add colour and flavour to your stews. Browning meat will caramelise the meat sugars, enriching the taste and enhancing the final dish.

Did you know...? For freshly minced meat, freeze sinew-free pieces (3 cm thick) of any kind of meat (e.g. beef, pork, lamb, turkey, chicken) in a single layer for 30-40 minutes. Mince the partially-frozen meat **10-15 sec/ speed 6**. Use your homemade minced meat for burgers, meatballs, meatloaf, bolognese sauce or *Shepherd's Pie*.

POULTRY

Poultry, such as chicken or turkey, is known for having a lower fat content than red meat. Nevertheless, the fat content of the final dish depends on its preparation method.

Poultry can be cooked as a whole bird, or as cuts such as breasts,

wings, legs, drumsticks or thighs. There are many ways to cook poultry with Thermomix®, depending on the cut of poultry and the type of dish. Steaming in the Varoma, browning or stewing are just a few of the different techniques you can use.

....

TIP | For a balanced diet, try to include a variety of different meat, fish, and meat-free dishes (refer to our Fish and Seafood and Meat-free Main Course Masterclasses on p. 106 and p. 96).

Did you know...? You can steam 800 g turkey leg in the Varoma dish for 80 minutes (use 1300 g water to steam). This technique of cooking slowly and at a low temperature will give you juicy and succulent meat.

TIP | SHREDDING MEAT
Place deboned, cooked meat without any sauce in the mixing bowl and shred **4-5 sec/↺/speed 4**. This is great for tacos, quiches, pies, or croquettes and is a good way to use up meat leftovers.

Buying Guide

Red meat should be bright red in appearance, while poultry should look pink or light red in colour, not too pale. The fat should be solid, and a healthy off-white colour. Store meat or poultry in the coldest part of the fridge, on the bottom shelf, for no more than 2 days. If you freeze it, cut into individual portions or in pieces as you wish to cook, then place in freezer-proof bags. Remove as much air as possible and seal tightly. To defrost, place in a container in the fridge to avoid the liquid dripping onto other ingredients. Never defrost meat at room temperature.

TIP | If you buy prepacked meat or poultry, always check the 'Use by' date. Choose the packets from the back of the shelves because these will typically be the newest ones.

COMBINING FLAVOURS

Some combinations of flavours are more well-known than others, and we tend to use those we are familiar with more often. Try experimenting with different spices, herbs, fruit or sauces to enhance your meat dishes. For example, beef stew can include ingredients such as mushrooms, beer, red wine or port, thyme, bay leaves, carrots and sautéed onions. A good steak, simply seasoned with salt, can be served with a rosemary butter and black or pink pepper, or with an easy *Béarnaise Sauce*.

In many countries, pork is cooked with sweet ingredients. Apples, pineapples or a combination of soy sauce and honey are classic combinations. Pork also works well with aromatic herbs such as sage, rosemary or thyme and with spices such as coriander seeds, cumin or star anise.

Lamb with mint is a classic combination, but it also pairs well with coriander and rosemary. Lamb cooked with spices is popular and in Middle Eastern cuisine, it's often cooked with fruit such as dried apricots. Peas, green beans and aubergine make lovely side dishes for lamb.

Chicken goes well with fresh, citrus ingredients such as lemon, basil or coriander. It's also delicious in a coconut curry sauce or with a mushroom and cream sauce. Tomatoes or mustard with orange are also good with chicken dishes.

Turkey goes well with bacon, sage, rosemary, thyme and garlic. A mixture of Chinese five spice, star anise, fennel, cinnamon and clove is great for rubbing on a turkey leg or a whole turkey.

Duck breasts with an orange or red berry sauce make for an impressive meal.

PREPARING CHICKEN

Chicken is one of the most widely-eaten foods in the world. This versatile meat is quick to cook and is typically popular with both children and adults. Use in recipes such as soups, stews, pies, and salads. Chicken takes on flavours very well, and is a lean meat that is great for steaming, stewing, baking, roasting, grilling or frying.

STUFFED CHICKEN BREASTS

Chicken breast is easy to prepare and commonly used in daily cooking. Add flavour to a chicken breast by stuffing it with different fillings. A mixture of butter, herbs, lemon zest and garlic works well, or try mozzarella cheese with spinach and sun-dried tomatoes.

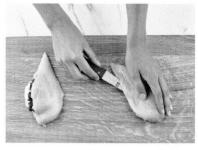

With a sharp knife, make a horizontal cut approx. 4 cm deep in the chicken breast, forming a pocket.

Fill the chicken breast with the stuffing of your choice and close with a cocktail stick or kitchen string.

DEBONING CHICKEN THIGHS

Chicken thighs are less expensive than breasts, but valued for being tastier. They have darker meat with more fat content, and are more succulent than the breast. Debone the chicken thighs, removing the skin, and cut into cubes for stews. Deboned thighs can also be stuffed. Try stuffing them with a mixture of chopped nuts, chopped parsley and raisins, or with a tapenade for a Mediterranean flavour.

Important

- To prevent cross-contamination, use hot water and soap to clean your knife, cutting board or any utensil that comes into contact with raw or cooked meat.
- Some meats, such as pork, turkey and chicken, are more susceptible to bacterial contamination. Ensure this meat is thoroughly cooked before serving.

Place the thigh on a chopping board, skin-side down. Use a small, sharp knife and insert next to the bone. Cut the meat close to the bone.

Do the same on the other side of the bone, then cut away the bone. Pull the skin away from the flesh.

TIP | Save the chicken bones and any skin in the freezer for making chicken stock later.

TOMATO AND BASIL
CHICKEN STEW

Another fabulous, easy, one-pot dinner for the
family. Serve this flavour-packed stew on its own
or alongside rice, potatoes or pasta with freshly
grated Parmesan scattered over to finish.

10 min   35 min

6 portions

Easy

Per portion: 324 kcal

Chicken, cannellini beans,
tomatoes, carrots, basil

PUY LENTIL AND SAUSAGE CASSEROLE ⊗ ⊗

✎ 5 min ⏲ 45 min

 4 portions

👨‍🍳 Easy

📊 Per portion: 364 kcal

🔑 Sausages, Puy lentils, carrots, fresh herbs; frying pan

Lentils are a great addition to any dish, providing plenty of protein and fibre. This recipe uses Puy lentils which are known for their nutty and slightly peppery flavour. For other lentil recipes, try *Lentil Moussaka*, *Steamed Pumpkin with Curried Lentils* or *Quick Lamb Dhansak*.

BEEF STROGANOFF

 25 min ⏱ 1 h

🍽 4 portions

👨‍🍳 Easy

📊 Per portion: 449 kcal

⚲ Beef, onions, mushrooms, meat stock, cream

Cooking this much-loved beef dish becomes easy thanks to the high cooking temperatures of Thermomix®. Simply serve with rice or tagliatelle.

CHINESE PORK WITH VEGETABLES

Chinese flavours are a crowd pleaser for family and friends, and popular with all ages. Stir-fry this tasty and colourful pork dish in your Thermomix® for a popular weekend lunch or a special dinner.

TM6
exclusive

- 45 min
- 1 h 20 min
- 6 portions
- Easy
- Per portion: 415 kcal
- Pork, dried rice noodles, vegetables, soy sauce, oyster sauce, chilli, garlic, ginger

Tailored to You

Lifestyle, ethics, body type and intolerances are just a few of the factors that impact food preferences. You may not enjoy the taste of green vegetables, you may be intolerant to gluten, or perhaps you've been advised against eating red meat. Many of us are now aware of the diet and nutrition that suit us best. Technology provides us with personalised health plans, based on our individual biology, medical history and lifestyle. Cooking your meals with Thermomix® means you'll have the satisfaction of being able to control exactly what you put into your body.

WHAT TO COOK?

First find your recipe on Cookidoo®, searching by dietary preference. Here are some of the most popular search terms:

- Low carb
- Gluten free
- Vegetarian
- Vegan
- Sugar free
- Dairy free

DINNERS FOR A DIVERSE CROWD

LOW CARB

Low-carbohydrate diets avoid sugary or starchy foods that can cause higher blood sugar levels and increase our insulin needs. A low-carb diet is usually higher in proteins, fat and low-carb vegetables. Most of us can easily identify high-carb ingredients such as grains, sugar, rice and potatoes. What's more challenging is to identify which vegetables are low in carbohydrates. Broccoli, asparagus, mushrooms, spinach, courgettes, cauliflower and peppers are all low-carb vegetables. Peas, corn, pulses and fruit in general have high levels of carbohydrates.

GLUTEN FREE

Gluten is a protein that can cause intestinal inflammation. Whether you are cooking for someone with coeliac disease, or for someone who has an intolerance to gluten, avoid recipes that contain wheat, wheat-derivatives (semolina, durum, spelt), wheat-based ingredients (breadcrumbs) or other grains containing gluten, such as rye or barley. Most packaging identifies whether the product contains wheat.

VEGETARIAN OR VEGAN

In Thermomix® recipes, we define a 'vegetarian' as an ovo-lacto vegetarian, meaning a Thermomix® vegetarian recipe will include no animal meat or fish, but may contain some animal products, such as eggs and dairy. Our vegan recipes exclude all animal products including meat, fish, dairy, eggs and honey.

Substitute ingredients. When a recipe you would like to cook does not meet your dietary requirements, consider replacing some of the ingredients. As always, making changes to a recipe can lead to unexpected results, but with experience you will learn what works and what doesn't. For instance, nut milks often replace dairy milk one to one in baking recipes so typically this change would be fine to make.

Make your own ingredients. Thermomix® can help you make many of your own allergy-free ingredients, such as gluten-free flour, egg-free mayonnaise and nut milks.

To each his own. If you are catering to different dietary preferences, consider serving a mezze-style dinner with a variety of dishes on the menu. Tapas-style meals like this are great for sharing with friends and will be simple to put together, thanks to Thermomix® providing an extra pair of hands in the kitchen.

Cashew nuts

Cornmeal

Rye flour

Basmati rice

ARTISAN PLANT PIZZA ⊘ ✓ ⊘

Homemade flours are easy to make with Thermomix®. In this recipe, you can grind spelt and buckwheat grains to create the flours for the pizza base yourself. Also try grinding nuts and pulses for a range of other uses.

⟋ 20 min ⏱ 35 min

🍰 2 portions

👨‍🍳 Easy

📊 Per portion: 387 kcal

🔑 Spelt flour, buckwheat flour, cashew nuts, tomato purée, vegetables; rolling pin, baking tray

ALLERGEN-FRIENDLY ROASTED BUTTERNUT SQUASH AND BLACK BEAN CHILLI

This vegan chilli provides plenty of nutrients and protein and can be served either on its own or with rice or a jacket potato. For a cooling finish to the meal, try making the *Vegan Strawberry Ice Cream*.

15 min   45 min

6 portions

Easy

Per portion: 292 kcal

Butternut squash, onions, chilli, chopped tomatoes, black beans; baking tray

ALLERGEN-FRIENDLY TUNA AND SUN-DRIED TOMATO COURGETTI

This light, gluten-free main course is quick to prepare and easily doubled to feed 4 people. Serve with *Gluten-free Focaccia Bread* made in your Thermomix® for a complete meal.

 10 min 🕐 10 min

🍲 2 portions

👨‍🍳 Easy

📊 Per portion: 379 kcal

🔑 Tuna, courgettes, sun-dried tomatoes

SALMON, QUINOA, FETA AND MIXED VEGETABLE SALAD

Quinoa is a fantastic source of protein. Try this dish with healthy omega 3-rich salmon, or our *Goat's Cheese and Caramelised Onion Quinoa Tart* on Cookidoo® for a vegetarian option.

30 min   50 min

6 portions

Medium

Per portion: 534 kcal

Salmon, quinoa, feta, fresh herbs, peppers, tomatoes, kale

Multi-level Cooking

Cooking on all four Thermomix® levels allows you to create an 'all-in-one' main dish, such as meat with a side of vegetables and potatoes. You can even use the levels to prepare a full three-course meal. Multi-level cooking makes it easy to cook both large and small quantities and make several dishes at the same time.

FOUR LEVELS OF COOKING

When water or any liquid that may generate steam (e.g. soup or sauce) are placed in the mixing bowl and Varoma temperature is selected, steam travels through all available holes to heat and cook any ingredients along the way. If the bottom of the simmering basket is immersed in the cooking liquid, ingredients in contact with the liquid will be boiled rather than steamed, which is perfect for cooking rice or fish without needing to stir it.

Save time: While cooking a soup, sauce or stew in the mixing bowl, you can add ingredients to the Varoma at the same time to cook or reheat them. Cook two dishes at once – dinner in the mixing bowl and lunch for the next day in the Varoma. Prepare a stew in the mixing bowl and an omelette on the Varoma tray, or steam fish with vegetables en papillote in the Varoma dish.

Steaming is often associated with healthy eating. This gentle cooking method maximises taste and colour, while preserving many of the vitamins and minerals in food. It is ideal for preparing rice, seafood, fish, meat and vegetables.

SMALL OR LARGE

Cooking on all four levels of Thermomix® can help you whether you are cooking for one, a family of four, or for a crowd.

Use the maximum capacity of the mixing bowl and Varoma to increase the quantity of the finished dish. For example, when preparing meatballs with tomato sauce, while the sauce is cooking in the mixing bowl you can have meatballs cooking simultaneously in the simmering basket, Varoma dish and Varoma tray. The full capacity of the Varoma allows you to cook up to 8 portions of fish, meat, eggs, chicken or vegetables. When cooking for one or two, the four levels are ideal for making a complete meal with a starter, main course, side dish and dessert.

LET'S GET COOKING

Place enough water or water-based liquid (e.g. stock or sauce) in the mixing bowl. Start with a minimum of 500 g water for 30 minutes steaming, and add another 250 g water for each additional 15 minutes.

Place ingredients in simmering basket and/or Varoma dish and tray, ensuring some holes remain unobstructed for steam to circulate. Cover with Varoma lid.

TIPS AND TRICKS

Spice rubs or paprika add colour and flavour to meat; seeds, cinnamon or dried fruit do the same for breads and cakes.

For **juicy browned poultry or meat**, pan-fry briefly before or after steaming. Line the Varoma tray with baking paper to catch juices, then use to make a delicious sauce.

TIP | Place the ingredients that take the longest to cook in the simmering basket. Place the fastest cooking dish or ingredient in the Varoma tray, where it is easy to remove and set aside when ready – or, alternatively, it is easy to add at a later stage to make sure the whole meal is ready at the same time. Cooking juices will drip down from the Varoma or simmering basket onto the ingredients below, which is great for adding flavour to rice or soup. If you prefer not to season your food this way, you can also separate dishes from each other: place them on a heat-resistant plate or in a jar, line the Varoma tray with baking paper or wrap the food in parcels of baking paper.

Select the cooking time according to the ingredients you are using and choose Varoma temperature when cooking on all four levels.

TIP | Cooking times depend on quantity, quality and size of ingredients (see Resources p. 223).

Did you know...? You can reheat leftovers in the Varoma. This is a gentle method that doesn't dry out food.

GNOCCHI WITH SAUSAGES AND STEAMED SPINACH, APRICOTS WITH HONEY AND WALNUTS

This quick recipe produces a tasty main and a healthy dessert for two. Delicate apricots are steamed over the gnocchi which are served with a tasty sausage sauce – two courses that are ready in 35 minutes.

 10 min 35 min

2 portions

Medium

Per portion: 1119 kcal

Gnocchi, sausages, apricots, mushrooms, spinach, Parmesan; baking paper

PEA AND GINGER SOUP, LEMON SALMON WITH BROCCOLI AND POTATOES

 15 min 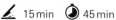 45 min

 4 portions

 Easy

 Per portion: 713 kcal

 Salmon, broccoli, peas, potatoes, cream

A quick, healthy meal full of bright flavours and colours, starting with a vibrant green pea soup with zingy ginger, followed by lemon-marinated salmon with steamed potatoes and broccoli. This multi-level recipe can turn a weeknight dinner into a special treat.

THREE COURSE MEAL FOR TWO: VEGETABLE SOUP, BAKED CHICKEN CASSEROLE WITH RICE, STEAMED CINNAMON APPLE

A full three course meal for two, easily created in your Thermomix® using the mixing bowl for soup, the simmering basket to cook rice, and the Varoma dish and tray for separating the main course from a tasty dessert.

- 20 min
- 1 h 15 min
- 2 portions
- Medium
- Per portion: 1010 kcal
- Chicken, vegetables, rice, milk; baking paper, baking dish

BREAD AND TOMATO SOUP, ROLLED SPINACH OMELETTE AND STEAMED RATATOUILLE VEGETABLES

A two course meal for four, all cooked at the same time in your Thermomix® – a delicious soup, followed by a beautifully steamed omelette with vegetables. Making two courses simultaneously couldn't be easier!

🔪 35 min   🕐 1 h 5 min

🍲 4 portions

🎚 Medium

📊 Per portion: 395 kcal

🔑 Tomatoes, spinach, cheese, bread, eggs, vegetables; baking paper

Weekend Time

Get Ahead

Hectic, modern lifestyles often leave little time to spend on meal preparation. This is where Thermomix® comes in, helping you make nutritious, great-tasting dishes that can be served straightaway or stored for later. Plan for good food and prepare ahead for those days when you are short of time. Let Thermomix® make it easy.

SAVING TIME

If you have a busy week coming up, you can prepare some recipes in advance to save time later on. Here are some tips to help you get a head start:

- **Marinades:** freeze raw meat in a marinade for up to 3 months. Defrost in the fridge for 24 hours. Once defrosted, the meat will be fully marinated and ready to cook.
- **Sauces/stocks:** after cooling, freeze in ice cube trays for 3-4 hours, then transfer to freezer bags to store.

- **Pizza bases/pastry:** roll out dough between sheets of baking paper. Freeze flat or roll up into a log, wrap in cling film and use within 3 months.
- **Individual portions:** single servings, such as fishcakes, can be made in advance, frozen uncooked and then baked or fried from frozen.
- **Bread dough:** see Fresh Bread Masterclass tips on p. 148 for fresh bread every day.

You can also cook entire meals ahead of time, then store in the fridge or freezer until needed.

- **Breakfasts and snacks:** make batches of granola, cereal bars and yoghurts. Freeze slices of bread or pancakes.
- **Versatile recipes:** choose recipes that can be used in different ways, such as a bolognese sauce or cooked, shredded chicken.
- **Recipes that freeze well:** soups, stews, casseroles and lasagne are popular recipes that can be frozen and reheated when needed. Freeze in muffin trays then transfer to freezer bags, so you can just remove the portions required.

TIP | Use the full capacity of your Thermomix® when cooking. Even if you don't need all of the food that day, you will have portions you can freeze for later.

FREEZING TIPS

TRAY FREEZING

Spread fruit and vegetables in a single layer on a baking tray lined with baking paper, freeze for 2-3 hours then transfer to freezer bags.

TIP | Ready to use – fruit and vegetables can be used without being defrosted in smoothies and soups.

Blanching vegetables before freezing

Green vegetables must be blanched before freezing to keep their colour and nutrients. Place 1000-1500 g water in the mixing bowl and heat water to 100°C. Add green vegetables, cut in pieces if necessary, to the mixing bowl and blanch for no longer than **3-4 min/100°C/speed 1**. Drain through Varoma dish and transfer immediately to a large bowl of iced water to stop the cooking. Squeeze if necessary, dry well, and leave to cool completely. Freeze the blanched green vegetables in small portions for up to 2-3 months.

INDIVIDUAL PORTIONS

Small airtight containers, muffin trays or ice cube trays are ideal for freezing individual portions. This avoids defrosting an entire batch of food and is quicker. You can also freeze sauces and blended fruit in this way.

PACKING AND LABELLING

Use freezer-proof bags or containers. Remove as much air as possible and seal tightly. Liquids expand when frozen so leave some space in the container.

TIP | Use different coloured labels to identify foods quickly. Include the name, date of freezing and quantity.

DEFROSTING

The safest way to defrost food is in the fridge. Defrosting fish or meat at room temperature can be dangerous as bacteria may develop on the outside of the ingredient before the inside is defrosted. Once defrosted, you can gently reheat dishes in your Thermomix®.

Important

- Allow your food to cool completely before freezing, to avoid raising the temperature in the freezer.
- Never refreeze previously defrosted food.
- In general, raw food can be frozen for up to 6 months and cooked food for up to 1-2 months.
- When reheating food, make sure it is reheated to a temperature of 70°C for 2 minutes so that it is completely hot throughout.

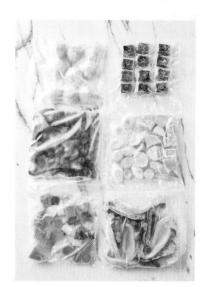

Freezing in plastic bags saves space in your freezer.

COTTAGE PIE

 25 min   ⏱ 1 h 10 min

🍽 4 portions

👨‍🍳 Easy

📊 Per portion: 755 kcal

🔑 Beef mince, onions, potatoes, milk; baking dish

Cook off the mince, whip up the mashed potato, then layer them in a dish and bake for a much loved recipe. This is a great one to make in advance and freeze for a convenient family meal for 4 people. Defrost in the fridge before reheating.

LAMB SPEZZATINO

This delicious, Italian stew is perfect to make in advance, then divide into portions for the freezer. Defrost fully before reheating and serve with cheesy polenta or mashed potatoes for an easy midweek meal.

 20 min 🕐 1 h 45 min

 4 portions

🍴 Easy

 Per portion: 393 kcal

 Lamb, fresh herbs, onions, bacon, chopped tomatoes, wine

CHICKEN CHIA BURGERS

These burgers are a great make-ahead option for a delicious midweek meal, or for adding to a weekend barbecue when extra guests arrive! For other great burger recipes, refer to Cookidoo®.

- 30 min
- 1 h 10 min
- 8 portions
- Easy
- Per portion: 292 kcal
- Chicken, carrots, courgettes, chia seeds, burger buns

BEEF AND ALE STEW

This rich, warming stew serves 6 people and is even more delicious the next day or after freezing when the flavours have had more time to develop. The constant, heat-controlled stirring provided by Thermomix® results in tender meat and a rich sauce.

🔪 20 min 🕐 2 h 20 min

🍲 6 portions

👨‍🍳 Medium

📊 Per portion: 394 kcal

🔑 Stewing steak, onions, beef stock, brown ale; large food bag, casserole dish

Fresh Bread

Nothing beats the taste and smell of homemade bread and with Thermomix®, making it is easy. If you are new to making bread you may have a lot of questions. What flour should you choose? Which yeast is best, and how much? When does the salt get added? Is it difficult to knead dough? What is the ideal oven temperature to bake bread? Here are our tips to guide you through the process so that you can enjoy fresh bread, every day!

MAIN INGREDIENTS

Basic bread is made from four ingredients: flour, yeast, salt and water.

WATER

The most widely used liquid to make bread is water. Milk can also be used and will produce slightly different results – typically a softer loaf, both in the crumb and the crust. Eggs can also be added to the dough to produce a richer bread, for example in brioche.

YEAST

Fresh yeast or dried yeast can be used to make bread. Most Thermomix® recipes give instructions for both.

TIPS

- **Fresh yeast** can be stored, wrapped in cling film, for up to 2 weeks in the fridge, or for up to 3 months in the freezer.
- **Dried yeast** should be stored in a cool, dry place. Once opened, seal it tightly, store in the fridge and use ideally within 4 months.
- Dried yeast can be **dried active yeast** or **dried instant yeast**. Dried active yeast has larger granules and needs to be dissolved in water before using, while dried instant yeast has a finer texture and can be mixed directly into dry ingredients. Thermomix® recipes use the instant variety.
- Dried yeast has three times more fermentation power than fresh. 20 g fresh yeast can be replaced by approximately 2 tsp dried instant yeast (8 g).

FLOURS

Strong wheat flour is the most popular for making bread because of the high gluten content. It is the gluten protein within flour that gives bread its structure and enables it to rise. However, bread can also be made from corn, rye, oats, spelt or any other cereal – including rice. When using other flours, it is a good idea to include some wheat flour in your bread dough to help create a lighter loaf.

TIP | MAKE YOUR OWN FLOUR
Grind whole grains in your Thermomix®
to make different wholegrain flours
for your breads (see Resources p. 223).

SALT

In addition to adding flavour, salt
helps strengthen the dough and
prevents it from collapsing while
baking. It also slows down the activity
of the yeast and ensures an even rise.
Avoid placing the salt in direct contact
with the yeast.

TIP | Use fine sea salt for best
incorporation into the dough.

OTHER INGREDIENTS

Doughs can be enriched with butter,
eggs, nuts, olives, dried tomatoes,
herbs, spices, olive oil, bacon, seeds,
oats, onions or garlic.

BREAD MAKING

MIXING AND KNEADING

When it comes to making bread, the
kneading process is essential for
activating the gluten in the flour.
Luckily, Thermomix® takes care of this
for you, with the dough mode saving
a lot of elbow grease!

TIP | Always add ingredients in the
order they are listed in the recipe.
If you want to add other ingredients
to flavour your bread, add them after
kneading then knead again for a few
seconds to incorporate.

RESTING AND PROVING

For rising, shape the dough into a
ball and place in a lightly greased
bowl. Cover with greased cling film
or a tea towel, and leave in a warm
and draught-free place until the dough
doubles in size (this time will vary
depending on the room temperature,
the ingredients and the amount of
yeast in the recipe).

TIP | To test if the dough is ready
to bake, gently press the dough
with your fingertip. The indentation
should disappear slowly. If the
dough springs up quickly, it has not
risen sufficiently. If the indentation
remains, the dough has over-proved.
The bread won't rise as much in the
oven but it will still taste good.

Shape the dough into the desired shape. Finish by slashing the surface, garnishing or glazing. Be careful to use a light hand to avoid knocking any air from the loaf.

FINISHING

Sprinkle with flour, brush with egg or milk, garnish with seeds, olives or herbs, or slash the top using a sharp knife. Whichever finish you choose, apply it carefully to avoid removing air from the dough.

TIPS | GLAZES AND TOPPINGS

- Apply the glaze thinly, using a pastry brush. Some options for glazes include:
  – water for a crisp crust;
  – milk or cream for a soft crust;
  – egg or egg yolk, whisked with a pinch of salt, for a shiny crust.
- Toppings such as wheat or barley flakes, oregano or rosemary leaves, sunflower, sesame or poppy seeds, grated cheese, chopped nuts and coarse salt can be sprinkled over glazed breads and rolls before baking.

Fresh bread every morning

To have fresh bread every morning, use less yeast (half the amount) and allow the dough to rise in the fridge, in a large bowl covered with greased cling film, for up to 3 days. For a simple bread, a slow rise in the fridge overnight gives the bread more flavour.

In the morning, take out enough dough for one roll (approx. 50 g). With floured hands, gently shape into a ball, taking care to keep as much air as possible in the dough, and place on a baking tray lined with baking paper. Preheat oven to 180-200°C for 10-15 minutes. The dough will rise while the oven is preheating. Bake for 15-18 minutes and enjoy the freshly baked loaf for breakfast.

SHAPING

When the dough has risen, tip out onto a lightly-floured work surface and knock back by gently punching out the air. Shape the dough into the desired shape(s) and place in tins or on a baking tray. Cover loosely with greased cling film or a tea towel and leave to rise until doubled in size again.

TIPS

- To form a smooth ball, tuck the sides of the dough into itself as if you were tucking socks into a ball.
- Wet and sticky dough can result in a beautiful open crumb with lots of even air pockets and a silky texture. You have to be careful that the dough doesn't stick to the surface or to your hands, but you also want to use as little flour as possible for a light result.
- Preheat the oven while the dough is rising.

Did you know...? To check if bread is cooked, remove from the oven and tap it underneath. If it sounds hollow, the bread is cooked through.

BAKING

For crusty loaves, high oven temperatures such as 240-250°C are usual, but the oven temperature must be adjusted based on the type of bread dough and size of the loaf. Refer to Thermomix® recipes to know which temperature is best for your specific bread, or follow these guidelines:

- **Rolls:** 180-200°C
- **Loaves:** for a thicker crust, bake bread at 240-250°C; for a thinner crust, bake at 180-200°C.
- **Breads with sugar or an egg glaze:** bake at 180°C to avoid burning the top.
- Creating a burst of steam produces a crisp, golden crust. Preheat two baking trays. As soon as you place the bread on the top baking tray, carefully splash a small cup of hot water on the lower baking tray and quickly close the oven. Alternatively, if available, use the steaming function of your oven according to the user manual.

Resist the urge to tear into the bread as soon as it comes out of the oven. For the best texture, leave it to cool on a wire rack to allow steam to escape and the cooking process to finish.

TIP | Steamed bread is delicious, quick to make in the Varoma and a nice alternative to baked bread. Look on Cookidoo® for our selection of steamed bread recipes.

RUSTIC BREAD

 20 min

⏱ 2 h

🍞 35 slices or 12 rolls

📊 Per slice: 70 kcal

👨‍🍳 Medium

🔑 Wheat grains, bread flour, yeast, buttermilk; large bowl, baking tray, baking paper

Make this versatile, rustic bread into a loaf for lunchbox sandwiches, make into small rolls for breakfast or serve a slice of a large, oval loaf topped with tomatoes as a bruschetta. Try different shapes, fillings or crusts – the possibilities are endless!

PITTA BREAD

Making homemade bread will save you money on your weekly food bill. This easy pitta bread recipe is fun to make – just watch the breads puff up in the oven as they bake!

🔪 15 min ⏱ 2 h

🍞 8 pieces

🎩 Medium

📊 Per piece: 238 kcal

🔧 Bread flour, yeast, rolling pin, baking tray

SANDWICH BREAD ⊘

Use this simple loaf for your lunchbox sandwiches,
or try the *Spelt Bread* or *Rye Bread Rolls* for other
possibilities. Thermomix® also makes great flatbreads;
simply search on Cookidoo® for inspiration.

🗡 10 min 🕐 3 h

🍞 24 slices

👨‍🍳 Easy

📊 Per slice: 90 kcal

🔑 Bread flour, yeast, butter;
loaf tin, large bowl

CHICKEN AND SPELT SALAD ⊠

Nutty spelt grains are cooked in the mixing bowl while juicy, tender chicken is steamed in the Varoma above. Complemented by pine nuts and brightened with fresh herbs and rocket, this is a substantial and hearty salad to enjoy for lunch or supper.

◢ 30 min ⏱ 1 h 15 min

🍽 6 portions

👨‍🍳 Easy

📊 Per portion: 292 kcal

🔑 Spelt grains, chicken, red peppers, rocket, pine nuts, fresh herbs; large salad bowl

TUNA AND SPRING ONION QUICHE

This light, flavourful quiche makes a tasty lunch, that can be enjoyed warm or cold. Try other quiches from Cookidoo® such as *Pumpkin, Leek and Lancashire Cheese*, or the classic *Quiche Lorraine*.

📐 15 min 🕐 2 h

🍲 8 portions

👨‍🍳 Easy

📊 Per portion: 594 kcal

🔑 Flour, butter, eggs, Cheddar, tuna, spring onions, crème fraîche; fluted tart tin, rolling pin, baking paper, baking beans

BEEF AND BEER PIE

This warming and cosy pie is perfect for
relaxed lunches. Browning the meat before
stewing gives a richer flavour to the pie.

TM6 *exclusive*

30 min   1 h 40 min

4 portions

Medium

Per portion: 647 kcal

Beef, onions, beer, flour,
butter; baking dish, rolling
pin, baking paper

TEX-MEX TORTILLAS AND SHREDDED PORK

 30 min  1 h 20 min

 6 portions

Easy

Per portion: 446 kcal

Pork, tomatoes, black beans, tortillas, avocado, jalapeños, red peppers

This tasty and colourful dish is easy to prepare and is a great choice for sharing with family or friends. Everyone can eat as much or as little as they like, and tailor their plate according to their preference.

TM6
exclusive

TOMATO RICE

For a nice variation on simple steamed rice, this tomato-flavoured version makes a tasty and colourful side dish. Enjoy with meat, fish or poultry.

 10 min   30 min

8 portions

Easy

Per portion: 241 kcal

 Rice, tomatoes, onions

MASHED POTATOES

The easiest mashed potato recipe, use floury
potatoes and the butterfly whisk to create this
light and creamy side dish that is loved by all.

 15 min 45 min

 4 portions

 Easy

 Per portion: 297 kcal

Potatoes, milk, butter, nutmeg

RATATOUILLE

This popular Mediterranean side is easy to make and delicious to eat. There are many interesting new side dishes available on Cookidoo®, such as *Creamy White Bean and Leeks* or *Coconut Creamed Kale*.

✎ 15 min   ⏱ 40 min

🍽 4 portions

👨‍🍳 Easy

📊 Per portion: 101 kcal

🔑 Tomatoes, red peppers, aubergines, courgettes

CAULIFLOWER CHEESE

Steamed cauliflower and the easiest all-in-one cheese sauce are combined to make this comforting and satisfying dish. Enjoy on its own or with your Sunday roast.

 10 min 50 min

 6 portions

 Easy

Per portion: 305 kcal

Cauliflower, milk, Gruyère; gratin dish

Ice Cream

When you have a Thermomix®, the only limitation to making ice cream is your imagination. This masterclass will show you how to make your own ice creams and sorbets without artificial colours and preservatives. Try adding fresh fruits, chocolate, nuts, caramel or even herbs to create exciting new flavours, and if you are watching your sugar intake, simply use less in your homemade frozen treats.

ICE CREAM AND SORBET

Ice cream is made with a base ingredient such as cream or milk, adding eggs for a luxurious taste. Recipes may include fruit, chocolate, nuts, caramel or other ingredients. Sorbet is usually fat-free and traditionally made from a mixture of fruit, syrup and/or flavoured water. Watermelon, strawberry, peach and lemon are popular sorbet flavours. Add herbs such as mint or thyme, or flavour with spices such as star anise or chilli.

....

TIPS | A common complaint about homemade ice cream is that it gets hard and icy when stored in the freezer. To help ice cream stay softer:

- For adults, add 1-2 Tbsp of an alcoholic drink such as a fruit liqueur (or vodka for a less alcoholic flavour).
- Sugar syrup, glucose, honey or golden syrup can all help achieve a softer consistency to your ice cream.
- **See tips for storage p. 173.**

Quick ice creams and sorbets

Fresh ice cream or sorbet is easy with a little preparation. Have frozen fruit, cut in pieces, ready in the freezer as well as frozen yoghurt or milk in cubes. When you want to make a super quick sorbet or ice cream, place sugar, to taste, in the mixing bowl and grind. Add your ice cream or sorbet ingredients, 70% of them frozen and 30% at room temperature. Blend with the aid of the spatula **1-2 min/speed 7-9** for a smooth ice cream or sorbet. Serve immediately.

MAKING ICE CREAM

THE CUSTARD BASE

Different bases can be used for making ice cream. In this masterclass, we will focus on a classic, versatile base used for *Vanilla Ice Cream – Crème Anglaise*. Also known as vanilla custard, it is made by gently cooking egg yolks with milk, cream, sugar and vanilla. Simply place all ingredients in the mixing bowl and Thermomix®, with its temperature-controlled settings, will cook the base perfectly for you. To freeze, pour mixture into shallow, freezer-proof containers (e.g. aluminium, silicone), up to 4 cm deep, then cover with cling film.

Allow mixture to cool completely for at least 10 hours before freezing.

TIPS | Use the *Vanilla Ice Cream* recipe as a base for:

- **Chocolate Ice Cream:** reduce egg yolks to 4, omit vanilla, and add 100 g grated chocolate and 50 g cocoa powder before cooking.
- **Caramel Ice Cream:** add 80-100 g caramel sauce to cooked vanilla custard. You can reduce the amount of sugar if desired.
- **Fruit (strawberry, mango, peach) Ice Cream:** omit vanilla and add 150-200 g fruit purée to freshly cooked custard. For a smoother result, cook and cool your fruit purée before adding to the custard.

CRUSHING

Once ice cream has frozen, cut into cubes (4 cm) with a sharp knife and crush in your Thermomix®, following the *Vanilla Ice Cream* recipe.

VANILLA ICE CREAM

📐 20 min

🕐 12 h

🍽 8 portions

👨‍🍳 Medium

📊 Per portion: 268 kcal

🔑 Milk, cream, sugar, egg yolks, vanilla pods; shallow freezer-proof containers, long sharp knife

Flavours

Mix-ins

After blending the frozen cream, add your favourite mix-ins, such as chocolate chips, honeycomb chips, peanut brittle or chopped nuts to the ice cream and fold them in with the spatula. Cover the surface of the ice cream with cling film and place in the freezer for 20-30 minutes before serving.

Swirls

Drizzle a spoonful of jam or sauce (e.g. chocolate hazelnut spread, caramel sauce or fruit coulis) into the bottom of a container, and spread a layer of ice cream over it. Add a few more spoonfuls of jam or sauce, then another ice cream layer. Continue the layering until all the ice cream is used. The sauce should not cover the whole layer. Use a knife to swirl the jam or sauce into the ice cream. Cover the surface of the ice cream with cling film and place in the freezer for 2-3 hours before serving.

SERVING

You can serve ice cream or sorbet immediately, or for a firmer consistency place in the freezer for 15-20 minutes.

TIPS | FOR STORAGE

- Pre-freeze storage containers before freezing the ice cream.
- Store ice cream or sorbet in shallow freezer-proof containers and cover the surface with cling film or a sheet of baking paper.
- Place in the coldest part of the freezer as quickly as possible.
- Ice cream is best eaten within one month.
- To serve, let the ice cream sit at room temperature for a few minutes to soften before serving in scoops.

Now you know how to make homemade ice cream, try different flavour combinations to create delicious frozen treats that will delight your friends and family.

TM6
exclusive

SALTED CARAMEL ICE CREAM

Perfect for summer treats, salted caramel ice cream can be served in many ways. Enjoy scoops in a cone, softly swirled into a sundae or sandwiched between cookies for an ice cream sandwich.

 25 min

 14 h

8 portions

Medium

Per portion: 486 kcal

Sugar, milk, cream, butter, egg yolks; shallow freezer-proof containers, long sharp knife, loaf tin

FROZEN FRUIT SORBET

A refreshing end to any meal, Thermomix® makes light work of preparing sorbets. Try our *Lemon* or *Papaya Sorbets*, or add a splash of alcohol to make *Champagne Grapefruit Sorbet*.

- 5 min
- 5 min
- 4 portions
- Easy
- Per portion: 133 kcal
- Mixed frozen fruit, sugar

PISTACHIO AND ALMOND GELATOS

✎ 20 min ⏱ 8 h 30 min

🍽 4 portions

👨‍🍳 Easy

📊 Per portion: 1177 kcal

🔑 Milk, sugar, pistachios, almonds;
shallow freezer-proof containers,
long sharp knife

Two deliciously nutty flavours in one recipe! Bring Italy to your
kitchen with this easy recipe for classic gelatos.

BERRY FOAM ⊘ ⚇ ⊗

The butterfly whisk helps to create the lightest, fruitiest frozen dessert. Ready in under 10 minutes, this is one that will impress family and friends.

✍ 10 min ◷ 10 min

🍲 8 portions

🍳 Easy

📊 Per portion: 100 kcal

🔑 Mixed frozen berries, sugar, egg white

FRUIT ICE CREAM

The quickest and easiest ice cream recipe, this is made using icing sugar ground in seconds with Thermomix®. There are plenty more ice cream flavours on Cookidoo®, from classic combinations to the more unusual and exotic.

✎ 5 min   ⏱ 5 min

🍰 6 portions

👨‍🍳 Easy

📊 Per portion: 134 kcal

🔑 Mixed fruit, cream, sugar

TIRAMISU

✐ 15 min   ⏱ 5 h 20 min

🍽 8 portions

👨‍🍳 Easy

📊 Per portion: 497 kcal

🔑 Mascarpone, sponge fingers, coffee; rectangular dish

A creamy custard and a light whipped cream layer, prepared easily with Thermomix®, are assembled to make this popular Italian pud. If you're looking for other desserts to impress, take a look at the array of classics from all over the world on Cookidoo®.

CHOCOLATE MOUSSE

Constant stirring while heating results in a reliable molten chocolate sauce, which is then folded into perfectly whipped cream to create a decadent dessert.

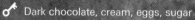

🖊 20 min   ⏱ 3 h 20 min

🍽 6 portions

👨‍🍳 Easy

📊 Per portion: 309 kcal

🔑 Dark chocolate, cream, eggs, sugar

RHUBARB CRUMBLE

A British classic that's best made in the Spring when rhubarb is in season. Swap the variety of fruit depending on the time of year: fresh berries in the Summer, apples, plums and pears in the Autumn. Alternatively, freeze fruits for whenever you crave delicious, homemade crumbles throughout the year.

✎ 10 min   ⏱ 55 min

🍽 6 portions

👨‍🍳 Easy

📊 Per portion: 420 kcal

🔑 Rhubarb, flour, sugar, butter; baking dish

LEMON
MERINGUE PIE 🌿

With all three layers made in your
Thermomix®, this impressive and
popular dessert is guaranteed to be
a hit every time.

📐 25 min   ⏱ 2 h 30 min

🍴 8 slices

🍴 Advanced

📊 Per slice: 521 kcal

🔑 Flour, butter, sugar, eggs,
lemons; tart tin, rolling pin,
baking paper, baking beans

BLUEBERRY AND MASCARPONE CHEESECAKE 🌿

There's a cheesecake for every occasion on Cookidoo®. Try the classic *Baked Vanilla*, or the steamed *Chocolate Chestnut Cheesecake*. This blueberry version only needs 15 minutes hands-on time and takes even less time to devour!

🔪 15 min   ⏱ 3 h 20 min

🍰 10 slices

👨‍🍳 Easy

📊 Per slice: 476 kcal

🔑 Blueberries, biscuits, mascarpone, condensed milk, lemon juice; springform tin, baking paper

STEAMED RASPBERRY JAM PUDDINGS

The Varoma makes steamed puddings simple. These individual servings also feature another Thermomix® great – homemade jam. Serve with freshly-made custard for a comforting dessert.

✎ 20 min ⏱ 1 h

🍽 8 portions

👨‍🍳 Easy

📊 Per portion: 292 kcal

🔑 Raspberry jam, flour, butter, sugar, eggs; dariole moulds, baking paper, foil

Sweet Baking

Whether it's for everyday bakes or special treats, you can rely on Thermomix® to produce fantastic results without fail. Here are some tips for success as well as some inspiration for your future bakes.

BAKING SUCCESS

BISCUITS

Often made in a single step, making biscuit dough with Thermomix® is fast and easy.

TIPS

- Refrigerate or freeze biscuit dough in a log shape wrapped in cling film. Whenever you need biscuits, simply slice off pieces (e.g. thick pieces for *Chocolate Chip Cookies*, or thin pieces of *Sweet Shortcrust Pastry*, for plain biscuits) and bake according to recipe.
- To make shapes, roll dough between sheets of baking paper then refrigerate for an hour – chilling the dough gives the shapes sharper edges. Remove the paper before using pastry cutters to create shapes.

BROWNIES

This rich treat is quick to make and great for feeding a crowd.

TIPS

- Line tin with baking paper, leaving some overhanging for easy removal.
- Add nuts, chocolate chips or a drizzle of caramel sauce to the mixture.
- For a quick dessert, serve brownies warm with vanilla ice cream.

CHOUX PASTRY

Profiteroles, éclairs or savoury cheese puffs: Thermomix® makes these classic pastries easy, even for beginners.

TIPS

- Pipe dough or drop spoonfuls of dough onto a tray. Pipe balls for profiteroles or sticks for éclairs.
- The pastries will puff up in the oven, leaving a hollow centre ideal for filling. Bake pastries until well browned so they do not collapse as they cool. Fill at the last moment so the pastry remains crisp.
- Choux pastries can be filled with whipped cream or pastry cream and served with fresh fruit, dusted with sugar.
- For a savoury version, fill choux pastries with cream cheese flavoured with fresh herbs.

MERINGUE

French meringue and Swiss meringue can both be made with Thermomix®. Ensure the mixing bowl is completely clean by rinsing with vinegar to remove all traces of fat, then rinse again with water and dry well. Make sure there is no egg yolk in the egg whites.

TIPS

- Draw shapes on a sheet of baking paper, turn over then pipe or spoon the meringue within the shapes.
- Crisp meringue must dry out for several hours at a low temperature (100-120°C). Meringue with a soft centre (e.g. *Peach Pavlova*) can be baked in less time and at a slightly higher temperature.

BAKING INGREDIENTS

- **Milk:** full fat or semi-skimmed.
- **Cream:** full fat (min. 30% fat).
- **Flour/plain flour:** white wheat flour (approx. 10-11% protein).
- **Sugar:** white caster sugar can often be replaced with raw, unrefined sugar.
- **Lemon/citrus fruit:** zest should be from wax-free fruit (organic if possible).
- **Vanilla sugar:** homemade, or shop-bought with natural vanilla.
- **Cocoa powder:** unsweetened.
- **Eggs:** medium size (53-63 g).

TIP | To avoid wasting any eggs, always separate each egg white into a small bowl first to check for any egg yolk before adding to the rest of the egg whites.

THERMOMIX® MASTERCLASS · THERMOMIX® MASTERCLASS

Cakes

A light and fluffy sponge cake forms the basis for layered birthday cakes, indulgent teatime treats and rich desserts. With Thermomix®, it is easy to make a perfect sponge cake. In this masterclass we take you through our top tips for successful cake making, as well as provide you with ideas for fillings and toppings.

INGREDIENTS

- If using food colouring for your icing, use natural colours such as beetroot, if possible. Alternatively, food colouring pastes will give a vibrant colour without affecting the texture of the icing, which can happen with more liquid-based food colourings.
- In a baking recipe, the precise combination of ingredients determines the result. Substituting or reducing ingredients will affect the finished dish. For instance, reducing sugar can affect not only the flavour but also the texture of the cake.

EQUIPMENT

- Scales, bowls and whisks are not needed; Thermomix® has them all.
- Using the size of tin that is specified in the recipe is important. Ideally it will have a removable base for easy unmoulding.
- To prevent the cake batter sticking, prepare the tin by greasing then lining with baking paper or sprinkling with flour. A paper-lined tin will produce a cake with less of a crust, whereas a greased and floured tin will result in more of a crust.
- A wire cooling rack is useful to turn the cake out onto.
- For icing or filling sandwich cakes, it is useful to have an angled or stepped palette knife.

- A piping bag is useful for producing beautiful toppings for your cakes. Small piping bags are easier to handle and essential for piping fine details such as writing, while bigger bags work well for decorating cupcakes or larger cakes.

....

TIP | If no piping bag is available, use a freezer bag with the corner cut off. Cut a tiny amount first, and increase if needed.

BAKING THE CAKE

- Always preheat the oven before you start a recipe.
- Follow the recipe for a guide to baking times. Oven temperatures are for fan assisted ovens and will need adjusting for conventional ovens.
- Ovens do vary in temperature and evenness of heat so using an additional oven thermometer is useful for checking the temperatures.
- Arrange your oven shelves so that cakes can be baked in the middle of the oven, where the temperature is even and air can circulate. If the temperature is too high, the crust will form before rising.

- If baking more than one tin, for a layered cake for instance, put the cake tins on the shelf next to each other. If they will not fit, put them on different shelves, but move them to each side, so that one is not directly over the other, enabling the air to circulate better.
- Cakes baked in tins made of thick or insulating material (e.g. ceramic, glass or silicone) usually require longer baking than those baked in metal tins.
- To test if the cake is done at the end of the advised cooking time, insert a skewer in the centre of the cake. If it comes out clean, the cake is ready.

- Turn the cooked cake out onto a wire rack to stop it cooking. To prevent the rack from making marks on the top of the cake, turn onto a board first, then flip onto the rack with the underside on the rack.
- Allow the cake to cool completely before cutting, decorating or filling.
- To divide a cake in two or more layers for filling, set on a board, take a bread knife and get down to eye level with the cake. Score the outside of the cake with a shallow cut all around the edge, while turning the cake. Keeping the knife horizontal, or parallel to the kitchen surface, keep turning and add gradual pressure to make the cut deeper, until you eventually slice the cake in half.

DECORATING – THE FUN PART

Buttercream and ganache are excellent for fillings or toppings and both work well for a simple sandwich cake. Before filling, set the bottom layer onto a serving plate, securing it with a teaspoonful of filling underneath. To avoid picking up any crumbs from the cake crust, spoon on the jam or filling in different spots across the cake, then use a table knife to spread out into an even layer.

For an icing, sugar glaze and chocolate icing such as ganache are easy favourites.

TIP | Sugar icing is a simple icing that can be spooned, and will dry with a nice opaque shine. It easily gives a nice finish to simple cakes such as *Yoghurt Cake* or *Lemon Cake*. For a natural pink colour, add a little strawberry juice.

FILLINGS AND TOPPINGS

- Popular fillings for cakes include fruit jam, lemon curd or whipped ganache and all are quick and easy to make with Thermomix®.
- For a special cake, use fresh fruit and whipped cream. Berries are ideal because they cut easily, or you can use other fresh, chopped fruit. Spoon or pipe the whipped cream across the base in an even layer, ensuring that the edges of the cake look attractive.
- Bananas and chocolate spread make a tasty filling for a chocolate cake.
- A cake filled with buttercream will need to be stored in the fridge. Remove 15 minutes before serving to bring back to room temperature.

TIP | Buttercream can be used both as a filling or a topping. It is a mixture of butter and icing sugar that can then be flavoured in a number of ways depending on your preference.

PIPING

- To fill a piping bag, place the piping bag in a wide jar or jug with the edges of the bag folded over the edge of the jar to keep it open.
- Spoon the icing or whipped cream into the bag, pushing it down towards the tip. Do not overfill, to keep the bag manageable. Twist the top of the bag shut.
- To pipe, squeeze the bag from the top, guiding the nozzle with your other hand. Take care to apply no pressure near the nozzle. Practice your piping on a plate then spoon the icing back into the piping bag before starting on the cake.
- When whipping cream for piping, take care not to over whip, or the cream may become grainy.
- If piping lettering, make plenty of icing and practice as needed until you feel confident to work on the real thing.
- Small errors can usually be corrected with a cocktail stick or small clean paintbrush.
- For an added effect, paint a line of food colouring inside the piping bag before filling with sugar glaze icing or buttercream.

• For the prettiest decoration, use a piping bag fitted with a star or other shaped nozzle.

....

TIP | Make a cake into a dessert by topping with billowy and soft whipped cream. Whip up in your Thermomix® using cold cream with a minimum fat content of 30% (e.g. whipping or double cream).

SPONGE CAKE

✎ 15 min

◔ 1 h 50 min

🍰 8 slices

🍳 Easy

📊 Per slice: 168 kcal

🔑 Eggs, sugar, flour; springform tin

This is a basic and versatile recipe that can be layered and sandwiched with fillings. It is perfect as a simple, everyday cake, or you can make it into a celebration cake by icing and decorating in a more elaborate way. The batter for this low-fat sponge is whisked at 37°C, creating a light and airy sponge. Alternatively, bake this cake as a sheet to use for Swiss rolls or layered mousse cakes.

BUTTER BISCUITS

A quick and easy biscuit recipe that can be flavoured to taste, try adding orange or lemon peel for a citrus twist, or ground ginger for a fiery treat.

🍴 20 min   ⏱ 50 min

🍰 30 pieces

👨‍🍳 Easy

📊 Per piece: 82 kcal

🔑 Flour, butter, sugar;
baking tray, baking paper

MARBLE CAKE

This and many other classic cakes can be found on Cookidoo®, all effortlessly mixed in your Thermomix®.

🔪 20 min   ⏲ 2 h 10 min

🍰 16 slices

👨‍🍳 Medium

📊 Per slice: 330 kcal

🔑 Flour, butter, sugar, vanilla, eggs, cocoa powder; bundt tin

BROWNIES 🌿

A family favourite made simple thanks to the controlled temperatures of Thermomix®. This ever-popular treat is one for chocolate lovers, and there are plenty of variations on Cookidoo®. Serve with a cup of tea mid-afternoon, or with ice cream for a rich and indulgent dessert.

🔪 10 min ⏱ 50 min

🍰 24 pieces

👨‍🍳 Easy

📊 Per piece: 229 kcal

🔑 Dark chocolate, butter, sugar, eggs, flour, walnuts; brownie tin, baking paper

LEMON DRIZZLE CAKE

 10 min 🕐 1 h 30 min

🍰 10 slices

👨‍🍳 Easy

📊 Per slice: 344 kcal

⚷ Lemons, sugar, butter, eggs,
flour; loaf tin, baking paper

A popular classic, this all-in-one sponge is drizzled with lemony syrup before serving. Perfect for a mid-morning or afternoon treat.

BLUEBERRY AND WHITE CHOCOLATE TRAYBAKE

Cookidoo® is full of inspiring cake recipes. Here, all of the preparation is done in your Thermomix®, from chopping the chocolate to making orange-flavoured sugar and mixing the batter together. A great option when feeding a crowd, the pop of colour and flavour from the blueberries is simply delicious.

✐ 20 min 🕐 1 h

🍲 20 pieces

👨‍🍳 Easy

📊 Per piece: 226 kcal

🗝 White chocolate, flour, butter, sugar, eggs, blueberries; square cake tin, baking paper

HOT CHOCOLATE

Made with real chocolate, this rich, velvety drink is a winner at any time of day. The benefit of making your own means you can use your milk of choice as well as adjust the sweetness.

 5 min   10 min

4 cups

Easy

Per cup: 249 kcal

Milk, chocolate

Special Occasions

Planning a Party

Getting organised and planning the details of your party in advance will avoid last-minute stress and ensure it is a success. Thermomix® will also be a great help when you are entertaining, making dishes easier and simpler to achieve. Here are some tips to plan for your next event at home.

4 STEPS FOR ORGANISING AN EVENT

1
YOUR GUEST LIST
Ask guests to RSVP and include a note of any dietary preferences ahead of time. This will enable you to plan a menu that fits in with your guests' needs.

TIP | For larger events or parties, send invitations at least one month in advance. This gives you sufficient time to prepare everything.

2
WHAT KIND OF PARTY IS IT?
Would you like to host a formal, sit-down dinner party or a more casual buffet meal? Think about the kind of atmosphere you would like to create for your gathering.

TIPS
• Formal dinners are great if you've got a group of around 4-8. Any more guests and you may find a buffet meal is a better option.
• Buffets work well for larger groups and can help to create a relaxed environment where everyone chats and mingles.

3
CHOOSE YOUR MENU
Once you are ready to plan your menu, Cookidoo® can provide you with recipe inspiration. Choose appetisers or starters, main dishes, side dishes, desserts and drinks. Search by number of portions, party recipes, season or type of celebration. Remember to include recipes for guests with specific dietary requirements.

TIPS

- Create a collection in Cookidoo® for all the recipes you will be making for your event. Bringing the recipes together will make it quicker for you when you come to cooking them, as well as enable you to easily create a shopping list.
- Do not plan for too many time-consuming recipes; choose one or two eye-catching dishes, and keep the rest simple.
- Choose dishes that can be left to cook in the oven or Varoma. Avoid recipes with too many last-minute steps.
- If you are making different dishes, remember that you don't need to provide a full portion per person. Have these guidelines in mind, per person: 150-200 g meat or fish, 60-80 g vegetables, 80-100 g potatoes or rice, 1-2 rolls or bread slice(s), 1 slice cake, 1 portion dessert.
- Make a note of recipes you can make ahead then refrigerate or freeze.

4
CREATE YOUR CHECKLIST

Careful organisation involves a lot of lists. Use our guide to create your own checklist.

Checklist

Two weeks before

- ○ **Check your cookware and tableware:** make sure you have enough glasses, dishes and cutlery.
- ○ **List the recipes that can be made and frozen in advance.**
- ○ **Create two shopping lists:** one with the ingredients for recipes you can prepare in advance and freeze, and another for the fresh ingredients needed the day before.
- ○ **Cook and freeze:** prepare dishes or parts of dishes that can be frozen.
- ○ **Start stocking your freezer with ice cubes.**
- ○ **Choose your playlist:** a key to the success of any party!

TIPS
- **Keep it casual:** A mixture of different glasses and plates gives your party a fun, casual feel.
- **Remember** napkins, useful items and decorative items such as candles or flowers.

Two days before

- ○ **Rearrange the room:** move furniture around if necessary.
- ○ **Cook and refrigerate:** dishes that will keep for two days in the fridge (e.g. marinades, sauces, cold desserts) or those that can be stored at room temperature in an airtight container (e.g. cookies or biscuits).

One day before

- ○ **Set the table or different areas:** place all the tableware, plates and cutlery in position. Decorate the room.
- ○ **Defrost:** place any dishes that you made ahead and froze in the fridge to defrost.
- ○ **Cook or prepare as much as possible:** prepare the baked dishes and the side dishes, decorate the party cake, chop ingredients, etc.

On the big day

- ○ **Drinks and salads:** make your cocktails or juices using Thermomix® to have drinks ready in no time at all. Chopped vegetable salad is prepared in minutes, and easy to eat standing up (as opposed to a leafy salad).
- ○ **Finalise your dishes:** pop your baked dishes in the oven, remove cakes from tins, dress salads, slice bread, etc.
- ○ **Light candles and turn on the music.**
- ○ **Enjoy the party!**

Making Your Recipes Wow

Thermomix® gives you the power to impress, making typically trickier recipes, such as soufflés, effortless. This gives you the confidence to go a step further and make those extra little touches and impressive finishes. Make your recipes WOW and share them with pride.

SAVOURY GARNISHES

- A simple yet effective presentation trick is to add height when plating your food. Make vegetable mash or creamed vegetables then spoon into greased dessert rings. Bake for 15 minutes at 180°C until the edges are golden. Turn out and serve as the base of your dish, then top with the meat, fish or vegetarian accompaniment.
- *Hollandaise Sauce* adds a luxurious touch to many simple dinners. Serve with fish or shellfish, steak, pork loin, steamed asparagus, potatoes, courgettes or broccoli. Impressive to serve, yet simple to make when you have Thermomix®! Add chopped herbs to the sauce and serve with steamed potatoes for a delicious, easy side dish.

- Drizzle the plate with a homemade pesto or sauce before serving, to add extra colour and flavour.
- For neat presentation, wrap portion-sized bundles of beans with a strip of prosciutto. Wrap in heat-resistant cling film and steam in the Varoma, then remove cling film just before serving.
- Make filo baskets from 3 squares of buttered filo pastry layered in a buttered muffin tin and bake for 10 minutes at 200°C. Spoon in cooked or roasted vegetables just before serving.
- Drizzle a few drops of cream or olive oil over soup, and sprinkle with herbs, bacon bits or croutons.
- Garnish the plate with lemon or lime slices or curls of lemon or lime zest.

TIP | To make spring onion flowers, make small cuts in an 8 cm piece of spring onion, cut from the thick end. Leave in water for at least 1 hour and a 'flower' will form.

SWEET GARNISHES

TIP | Use a large cookie cutter ring to create a nicely-presented salad. Set on the plate just before serving, and spoon in dressed green salad. Remove the ring and the salad will stay piled in place. Spoon the other elements on to the plate and serve.

ADDING A TWIST

Some easy ideas to present your dishes to impress your friends and family:

- serve layered desserts in pretty glasses with a decorative top;
- serve individual small tartlets instead of a single large tart;
- serve your soup, starter or cheese course with homemade bread and butter.

- For extra special occasions, top a chocolate cake with *Honeycomb* made in your Thermomix®.
- Drizzle *Caramel Sauce* onto the plate before adding your dessert. On a separate plate, sift icing sugar over some sprigs of mint. Use these to decorate the dessert for a restaurant-style finish.
- Serve a Thermomix®-made *Sabayon Sauce* with ice cream to make a show-stopping dessert.
- Pipe melted chocolate in pretty shapes on baking paper and refrigerate. Peel off and use to decorate your cake.
- Swirl a caramel sauce on top of an iced cake, or allow hard crack caramel to cool on baking paper, then break into shards to top the cake.
- Take two small paper cake cases per person, one inside the other, and turn upside down on a plate. Drizzle liquid caramel over and allow to cool and harden. Just before serving, remove the paper cases to reveal a caramel basket. Fill with whipped cream or ice cream and serve as soon as possible.
- Fresh fruit toppings make a simple cake special. Arrange raspberries or sliced strawberries in a pattern on the top.
- Arrange edible flowers over the top of a cake for a stunning summery presentation.
- Grind pistachios, for a green finish, or dried raspberries for a red finish, with sugar in your Thermomix® until very fine. Lay strips of baking paper across the cake to make neat lines, then sieve the sugar mix over the cake.

INDIVIDUAL BEEF WELLINGTONS WITH RED WINE JUS

Make light work of this impressive dish – all components are easily made in your Thermomix®. From crisp, buttery pastry to the rich mushroom duxelle that covers succulent beef fillet, your friends and family will all enjoy this luxurious main course.

⚖ 40 min ⏱ 2 h 10 min

🍽 4 portions

♟ Advanced

📊 Per portion: 967 kcal

🔑 Beef fillets, mushrooms, Madeira, flour, butter, eggs, port, red wine; frying pan, rolling pin, baking tray

COURGETTE AND AVOCADO BEIGNETS WITH FETA CREAM, CORIANDER CHILLI PESTO AND SALAD

Making choux pastry is fast and easy in your Thermomix®. Used here to make mini savoury doughnuts, this beautiful and colourful dish bursts with flavour. Ideal served as a starter or light lunch.

🔪 50 min   ⏲ 2 h 15 min

🍽 8 portions

👨‍🍳 Advanced

📊 Per portion: 529 kcal

🗝 Courgettes, avocado, spring onions, coriander, feta, yoghurt, cream; deep fat fryer, slotted spoon

BERRIES AND CREAM LAYER CAKE 🌿

Layer cakes are so impressive to look at, yet simple to make. Cookidoo® has many show-stopping cakes for every occasion, including *Triple Chocolate Layer Cake*, *Cappuccino Cake* and even an *Ice Cream Layer Cake*.

🔪 30 min ⏱ 2 h 15 min

🍰 12 slices

👨‍🍳 Medium

📊 Per slice: 419 kcal

🔑 Eggs, flour, sugar, cream,
fresh berries; springform tins,
baking paper

BITTER CHOCOLATE AND ORANGE LIQUEUR TART WITH HONEYCOMB DUST

Pastry is so easy in your Thermomix® and this version, with a hint of orange, is no exception. Filled with a silky smooth and luxurious centre offset by bitter chocolate, and finished with a crunchy honeycomb garnish, this recipe is sure to wow.

✎ 30 min ⏲ 3 h 45 min

🥧 12 slices

👨‍🍳 Medium

📊 Per slice: 617 kcal

🔑 Flour, butter, sugar, eggs, cream, orange liqueur, dark chocolate, honeycomb; tart tin, rolling pin, baking paper, baking beans

SOFRITO TOASTS WITH SERRANO HAM

A colourful and tasty canapé, these bites are super easy to put together. Consisting of a rich tomato layer topped with salty ham, these can be made ahead of time then chilled until needed.

🔪 5 min   ⏱ 40 min

🍽 30 portions

👨‍🍳 Easy

📊 Per portion: 49 kcal

🗝 Chopped tomatoes, onions, ham, baguette

CHESTNUT AND CRANBERRY STUFFING

Mix all the ingredients for this stuffing together in a matter of minutes before shaping into balls and baking in the oven. For this and other Christmas staples, visit Cookidoo®.

- 10 min
- 1 h 55 min
- 8 portions
- Easy
- Per portion: 309 kcal
- Sausagemeat, cranberries, port, chestnuts, fresh herbs; roasting tin

SALMON EN CROUTE WITH LEMON RISOTTO

This pastry log encases a classic, creamy salmon and dill filling. Served with a simple lemon-flavoured risotto, this is an impressive main course for a weekend dinner party.

🔪 25 min ⏲ 45 min

🍽 6 portions

👨‍🍳 Easy

📊 Per portion: 763 kcal

🔑 Puff pastry, salmon, cream cheese, lemons, Parmesan, risotto rice; baking tray, pastry brush

HOT CROSS BUNS

These fruity, sticky delights will be enjoyed by all at Easter. For more Easter inspiration, take a look at Cookidoo® and let Thermomix® help you prepare for even the largest family get-together.

🔪 30 min   ⏱ 3 h 50 min

🍲 16 pieces

👨‍🍳 Medium

📊 Per piece: 238 kcal

🗝 Milk, bread flour, spices, dried fruit, mixed peel; large bowl, roasting tin, piping bag

MINCEMEAT AND ALMOND TART

The flavours of Christmas shine through in this sweet tart. Rich, crumbly pastry is made in seconds before being filled with mincemeat and topped with almond frangipane.

⚖ 15 min ⏱ 2 h 15 min

🍰 12 slices

👨‍🍳 Medium

📊 Per slice: 574 kcal

🔑 Mincemeat, flour, butter, sugar, almonds, eggs; rolling pin, tart tin, baking paper, baking beans

QUICK CHRISTMAS CAKE

Full of fruit and spice, Thermomix® makes this last-minute cake so easy to prepare. Check out our many other Christmas recipes for even more inspiration when preparing for the big day.

 5 min 2 h 25 min

12 slices

Easy

Per slice: 334 kcal

Dried fruit, brandy, flour, sugar, butter, almonds; springform tin, baking paper

LEMONADE

A refreshing drink perfect for a warm day, the simmering basket is used as the strainer to remove all the lemon pieces. Many more delicious drinks are available on Cookidoo®.

- 5 min
- 5 min
- 6 glasses
- Easy
- Per glass: 76 kcal
- Lemons, sugar, ice; jug

STRAWBERRY FLUTE

A versatile recipe that can be made with raspberries instead of strawberries or as a non-alcoholic version, this summery drink is ready in under 5 minutes. The power of Thermomix® means you can use frozen fruit , resulting in a chilled cocktail everyone will enjoy.

🔪 5 min ⏱ 5 min

🍮 6 glasses

👨‍🍳 Easy

📊 Per glass: 147 kcal

🗝 Strawberries, grenadine, sparkling wine

CUCUMBER GIN GRANITA ⊘ ✓ ✗ ▯

Make a mint-infused homemade syrup before blitzing it with ice in your Thermomix® for a modern take on this popular cocktail.

◢ 5 min ⏱ 45 min

🍽 8 glasses

👨‍🍳 Easy

📊 Per glass: 122 kcal

🔑 Gin, cucumber, sugar, fresh mint, ice

COSMOPOLITAN

Thermomix® is great for whipping up classic cocktails like this. Search on Cookidoo® for Bellini, Mojito or Daiquiri recipes to find something to your taste.

🔪 10 min   ⏱ 10 min

🍽 4 glasses

👨‍🍳 Easy

📊 Per glass: 273 kcal

🔑 Vodka, orange liqueur, cranberry juice; cocktail glasses, baking tray, kitchen blowtorch

Caramel

Successfully making caramel the traditional way requires patience, skill and experience. The sugar and water must be heated at the right temperature for the right amount of time, with careful attention and limited handling. At the end, if the day is not too humid, the result will be a delicious, golden brown caramel. Thermomix® takes the guesswork out of cooking caramel. By controlling time, temperature and speed for you, Thermomix® produces perfect results every time. Try our caramel ideas to make your special occasions sweeter.

CARAMEL

Caramel is simply caramelised sugar. During heating, the sugar reaches different cooking stages: a simple syrup to use in ice creams; hard crack stage which is good for lollipops or candies; pale or light amber caramel to decorate a cake or for the magnificent French dessert Croquembouche; dark amber caramel, to line a tin for a caramel flan. A darker caramel will taste more bitter and will be harder than a lighter one.

In general, caramel can be made with two different methods: the wet method where sugar is cooked with some liquid, or the dry one where sugar is caramelised without any liquid. Thermomix® recipes use the wet method to produce consistent results.

TIP | White sugar is commonly used to make caramel. However, you can also use other sugars, such as Demerara, light brown sugar or dark brown sugar. These sugars have more complex aromas and flavours than the white variety and produce a darker and deeper flavoured caramel.

To avoid crystallisation and spoiling the caramel, certain ingredients can be used to stabilise the sugar, such as lemon juice, cream of tartar, glucose, inverted sugar, honey or golden syrup. Some may interfere with the colour, which is why each Thermomix® recipe specifies which one is needed. Follow the recipe for perfect results.

COOKING WITH SUGAR

Thermomix® high temperature sugar recipes can be combined with other dessert recipes for extra panache.

LOLLIPOPS

To make lollipops, the hard crack stage (approx. 150°C) must be reached. The cooked sugar becomes translucent and cracks when it cools. Lollipops can be made in different shapes. Use moulds or simply pour the syrup onto an oiled or baking paper-lined heat-resistant surface and leave it to set.

Cover fruit, such as strawberries or apple balls shaped with a melon ball scoop, with the hot syrup, and set aside over a wire rack to cool. Insert a cocktail stick into each piece of fruit to make it easier to handle.

TIP | ROCK CANDY
Add 1-2 tsp flavouring extract to taste before cooking the lollipop recipe. The exact quantity depends on the flavouring you are using (peppermint and cinnamon are generally much stronger than other flavourings).

The candy syrup will reach a high temperature. Line a baking tray or heat-resistant tray with baking paper. Carefully pour the hot syrup onto the baking paper and allow to cool and harden before breaking into pieces and covering with icing sugar. Store in an airtight container for up to 3-4 days.

CARAMEL SAUCE

Caramel enriched with butter and cream stays liquid and thick. Turn simple ingredients into weekend treats with this delicious caramel sauce – use as:

- a topping – for pancakes, ice creams, éclairs or profiteroles;
- a filling – for brownies, chocolate chip cookies, cakes or tarts;
- an ingredient – for caramel buttercreams, caramel milkshakes, hot caramels or salted caramel ice creams.

For a different flavour, add salt, ground cardamom seeds, bourbon or vanilla extract to your caramel sauce (refer to the tips in the recipe).

TIP | TOFFEE APPLES
Place 6-8 small Granny Smith apples in a large bowl and cover with boiling water. This will remove the waxy coating and help the caramel to stick. Dry thoroughly.
Line a baking tray with baking paper and push a wooden skewer into each apple. Omit the last step of the caramel sauce recipe and dip each apple immediately in the hot caramel sauce. Place on the prepared baking tray and leave to set before serving.

PEANUT BRITTLE

This easy and crunchy nut brittle can be made with different nuts or seeds. For a richer flavour, toast the nuts in the oven before using them. To sprinkle over desserts, chop or grind with Thermomix® using the basic functions.

TIP | CARAMEL POPCORN
Line a baking tray with baking paper and spread 150 g salted popcorn over it. Add ½ tsp bicarbonate of soda to the hot caramel, stir with the spatula and pour immediately over the popcorn. Mix with the spatula and spread on the baking tray. Allow to cool completely before serving.

MAKING HONEYCOMB

INGREDIENTS

Caramelised sugar and honey give this porous brittle its distinctive flavour. Bicarbonate of soda is the secret to achieving an airy texture. It is fun to make and kids will love to watch.

LET'S START

Place sugar, water and honey in mixing bowl and, without measuring cup, start cooking.

TIP | Honey can be replaced with golden syrup.

Meanwhile, line a square baking tin (18 cm) with baking paper. Have 1 tsp bicarbonate of soda ready. When cooking time ends, immediately sprinkle bicarbonate of soda around the mixing knife, to ensure even distribution then stir with spatula to create a foam. Transfer mixture immediately to prepared baking tin. Leave to cool completely at room temperature before breaking into pieces. Use as desired.

TIP | Store honeycomb in an airtight container and serve within a few days before it gets sticky. For a longer shelf life, coat completely in chocolate.

Important for all caramel recipes

- Handle the hot caramel carefully.
- As soon as you finish the caramel recipes, immediately use the cleaning mode. If the caramel cools and hardens in the mixing bowl, fill the mixing bowl with hot tap water and allow to soak until all the caramel is dissolved, then clean as usual.
- Humidity is caramel's number one enemy. Store your caramel sweets in an airtight container in a cool place to prevent them from absorbing moisture. Use as soon as possible.

 TM6 *exclusive*

HONEYCOMB

 10 min

🕐 1 h 30 min

🍮 Approx. 40 pieces

👨‍🍳 Medium

📊 Per piece: 32 kcal

🗝 Honey, sugar, bicarbonate of soda; baking tin, baking paper

Honeycomb is a delectable treat and great for decorating or adding to desserts. Serve sprinkled over ice cream or a layered chocolate cake.

CARAMEL TOFFEES

Homemade toffees are successful every time in Thermomix®. Wrap them up in pretty paper to make great gifts for birthdays, Christmas or for your teacher.

 30 min 2 h

75 pieces

Medium

Per piece: 37 kcal

Sugar, cream, butter, lemon juice; baking tin, baking paper

PEANUT BRITTLE

Make confectionery at home with all-natural ingredients as an alternative to shop-bought sweets. This simple, sweet treat can be made your own by adding sesame seeds, dried strawberries or flaked coconut.

TM6
exclusive

🖊 10 min ⏱ 1 h 30 min

🍰 30 pieces

♟ Easy

📊 Per piece: 51 kcal

🔑 Sugar, butter, lemon juice, peanuts; baking tin, baking paper

Resources

Chopping Functions

Use this table as a guide for chopping your ingredients. Ingredient quantities can be adjusted as needed, while for some ingredients (e. g. nuts), the results will be more consistent if you chop in several batches instead of increasing the quantity. When a range is provided, use the longer time for a finer chop or grind.

GRATING

FOOD	AMOUNT	TIME/SPEED	TIPS AND TECHNIQUES
Carrots, turnips, daikon	100-180 g, cut in pieces (4 cm)	**3-4 sec/speed 5**	
	200-450 g, cut in pieces (4 cm)	**4-6 sec/speed 5**	
	500-700 g, cut in pieces (4 cm)	**5-7 sec/speed 5**	
Cabbage (white/red) - finely grated	200-400 g, cut in pieces	**6-8 sec/speed 5**	
Cabbage (white/red) - coarsely grated	200-400 g, cut in pieces	**2-4 sec/speed 5**	
Apples	100-300 g, quartered	**2-3 sec/speed 4.5**	
	350-600 g, quartered	**3-4 sec/speed 4.5**	
Plums, medium ripeness	200-300 g, quartered	**3-5 sec/speed 4.5**	
	350-600 g, quartered	**4-6 sec/speed 4.5**	
Pears, nectarines, apricots, medium ripeness	200-300 g, quartered	**3-5 sec/speed 4.5**	
	350-600 g, quartered	**4-6 sec/speed 4.5**	
Dark chocolate - coarsely grated	70-200 g, cut in pieces	**3-4 sec/speed 7**	• For thick bars of chocolate, use the longer time, adding **1-2 seconds** as needed.
	250-300 g, cut in pieces	**4-5 sec/speed 7**	
Milk chocolate - coarsely grated	70-100 g, cut in pieces	**3-4 sec/speed 6**	• For thick bars of chocolate, use **speed 7**.
	150-200 g, cut in pieces	**4 sec/speed 6**	
	250-300 g, cut in pieces	**4-5 sec/speed 6**	
White chocolate - coarsely grated	70-200 g, cut in pieces	**2-3 sec/speed 7**	• For thick bars of chocolate, use the longer time, adding **1-2 seconds** as needed.
	230-300 g, cut in pieces	**4 sec/speed 7**	
Dark chocolate - finely grated	70-200 g, cut in pieces	**10-12 sec/speed 8**	
	250-300 g, cut in pieces	**12-15 sec/speed 8**	

GRATING, *continued*

FOOD	AMOUNT	TIME/SPEED	TIPS AND TECHNIQUES
Milk chocolate – finely grated	70-200 g, cut in pieces	**6-7 sec/speed 8**	
	250-300 g, cut in pieces	**7-9 sec/speed 8**	
White chocolate – finely grated	70-200 g, cut in pieces	**6-8 sec/speed 8**	
	250-300 g, cut in pieces	**8-9 sec/speed 8**	
Breadcrumbs – coarse	100 g bread, fresh, cut in pieces (3 cm)	**3-10 sec/speed 6**	• Use white or crusty bread such as baguette, ciabatta, whole wheat bread or bread rolls. • Add herbs or garlic to the bread before grating. • Breadcrumbs made from fresh bread must be stored in the freezer.
Breadcrumbs – fine	100 g bread, cut in pieces (3 cm)	**7-20 sec/speed 7**	
Potatoes and sweet potatoes	200-500 g, cut in pieces	**4-7 sec/speed 5**	• Chopping time depends on type of potatoes.
	600-800 g, cut in pieces	**5-10 sec/speed 5**	
Cheese, medium-hard (e.g. Gruyère, Cheddar, Emmental)	70-300 g, cut in pieces (2-3 cm)	**5-14 sec/speed 7**	
Parmesan cheese (or other hard cheese)	50-70 g, cut in pieces (2 cm)	**10 sec/speed 10**	• Remove crusts before grinding.
	100-250 g, cut in pieces (2 cm)	**12-20 sec/speed 10**	

CHOPPING/CRUSHING/MINCING

FOOD	AMOUNT	TIME/SPEED	TIPS AND TECHNIQUES
Fresh herbs (e.g. parsley, coriander, sage, thyme, mint)	5 g, leaves only	**3-4 sec/speed 6**	• Make sure leaves are dry for best chopping results.
	10-25 g, leaves only	**4-6 sec/speed 6**	
	20-30 g, leaves only	**3-4 sec/speed 7**	
	30-40 g, leaves only	**5-9 sec/speed 6**	
Dill	5-40 g, leaves only	**4 sec/speed 8**	• If further chopping is required, scrape down sides of mixing bowl with spatula and chop again **2 sec/speed 8**.
Rosemary	5-30 g, leaves only	**10 sec/speed 8**, scrape down sides of mixing bowl with spatula, then chop again **5 sec/speed 8** if necessary	• Moisture content of rosemary is variable.
Garlic	1 clove	**2 sec/speed 8**	
	10-20 g	**3 sec/speed 8**	
	25-70 g	**3 sec/speed 5**	
	100 g	**3-5 sec/speed 5**	
Onions	30-70 g, halved	**3-4 sec/speed 5**	• Cut large onions in quarters.
	100-200 g, halved	**4 sec/speed 5**	
	220-350 g, halved	**4-5 sec/speed 5**	
	400-500 g, quartered	**5-6 sec/speed 5**	
Crushed ice	200-550 g ice cubes	**3-8 sec/speed 5**	• The length of time depends on size of ice cubes and desired result. • The quantity of ice can be increased as long as ice cubes do not exceed the 1 litre mark in the mixing bowl.
Beef	300 g, cut in pieces (3 cm), partially frozen	**10-13 sec/speed 8**	• To achieve a uniform result, cut meat in equal-sized pieces. • The best result is achieved with meat that is partially frozen for 60 minutes. However, make sure it is only partially frozen.
	500 g, cut in pieces (3 cm), partially frozen	**13-16 sec/speed 8**	

FOOD	AMOUNT	TIME/SPEED	TIPS AND TECHNIQUES
Pork	300 g, cut in pieces (3 cm), partially frozen	**8-10 sec/speed 6**	• To achieve a uniform result, cut meat in equal-sized pieces.
	500 g, cut in pieces (3 cm), partially frozen	**12-14 sec/speed 6**	• The best result is achieved with meat that is partially frozen for 60 minutes. However, make sure it is only partially frozen.
Poultry (white meat)	300 g, cut in pieces (3 cm), partially frozen	**5-6 sec/speed 6**	
	500 g, cut in pieces (3 cm), partially frozen	**7-8 sec/speed 6**	
Lamb	300 g, sinew free, cut in pieces (3 cm), partially frozen	**10-13 sec/speed 8**	
Nuts (e. g. almonds, hazelnuts) - coarsely chopped	100 g	**3-5 sec/speed 6**	
	200-300 g	**4-6 sec/speed 6**	
Nuts (e. g. peanuts, cashew nuts) - coarsely chopped	100-200 g	**3-6 sec/speed 5**	
	300 g	**2-5 sec/speed 5**	
Nuts (e. g. walnuts, pecans) - coarsely chopped	100 g	**2-6 sec/speed 4**	
	200 g	**3-7 sec/speed 4**	
	300 g	**1-3 sec/speed 5**	

GRINDING / MILLING

FOOD	AMOUNT	TIME/SPEED	TIPS AND TECHNIQUES
Nuts (e.g. walnuts) - finely ground	100 g	4-6 sec/speed 6	
	150-250 g	5-7 sec/speed 6	
Nuts (e.g. almonds, hazelnuts, cashew nuts, peanuts) - finely ground	100 g	6-8 sec/speed 7	
	150-250 g	6-10 sec/speed 7	
Dried pulses (e.g. chickpeas, lentils, dried beans) - finely ground	100 g	20-50 sec/speed 10	• For best results, grind up to 250 g at a time. If more flour is needed, repeat the process in batches of up to 250 g.
	150-250 g	30-60 sec /speed 10	• Time depends on type of pulse.
Cereal grains (e.g. wheat, rye, spelt, buckwheat, millet) - finely ground	100 g	10-50 sec/speed 10	• Cereal grains can be ground coarsely or very fine (flour). The longer the grinding time, the finer the grind.
	150-250 g	15-60 sec/speed 10	• For best results, grind up to 250 g at a time. If more flour is needed, repeat the process in batches of up to 250 g.
Coffee beans	100-250 g	1 min/speed 9	
Poppy seeds	100-250 g	30 sec/speed 9	
Peppercorns – coarse	10 g	10 sec-1 min/speed 10	
Rice	100-150 g	1 min-1 min 30 sec/ speed 10	
Sesame seeds	100-150 g	6-10 sec/speed 9	• Use unpeeled sesame seeds for fine flour, and peeled sesame seeds for sesame seed paste.
	160-200 g	9-15 sec/speed 9	
Spices	20 g	20-60 sec/speed 9	• Grinding time depends on the spices used.
Icing sugar (white, brown and dark brown)	100 g	11-14 sec/speed 10	• For best results, grind sugar in 100-200 g batches.
	150 g	15-18 sec/speed 10	
	200 g	17-20 sec/speed 10	

Steaming Functions

Use this table as a guide to steaming times, adjusting amounts and times according to your preference. Cooking times will vary depending on the quantity, size and temperature of ingredients. To extend cooking time beyond 30 minutes, add 250 g water for each additional 15 minutes. Make sure a few holes in the Varoma dish and Varoma tray remain unobstructed, and that the Varoma lid is properly closed.

Place 500 g room temperature water or broth in the mixing bowl and steam **stated time/Varoma/speed 1**.

STEAMING VEGETABLES

FOOD	AMOUNT	TIME	TM PART	TIPS AND TECHNIQUES
Carrots	200-500 g, sliced (5 mm)	**18-24 min**	Simmering basket	
	550-800 g, sliced (5 mm)	**25-30 min**	Varoma	
	300-1000 g, thin, whole	**25-30 min**	Varoma	
Parsnips	200-500 g, peeled, cut in bite-sized pieces	**10-15 min**	Simmering basket	• To achieve uniform results, cut parsnips in equal-sized pieces.
	600-1000 g, peeled, cut in bite-sized pieces	**15-20 min**	Varoma	
Kohlrabi, turnips, daikon	200-600 g, cut in pieces (2-3 cm)	**18-25 min**	Simmering basket	
	700-1000 g, cut in pieces (2-3 cm)	**24-30 min**	Varoma	
Broccoli florets	250 g	**11-15 min**	Simmering basket	
	400-800 g	**15-22 min**	Varoma	
Cauliflower florets	300 g	**15-20 min**	Simmering basket	
	400-900 g	**20-25 min**	Varoma	
Cabbage	300 g, cut in strips (1-2 cm)	**10-15 min**	Simmering basket	
	400-800 g, cut in strips (1-2 cm)	**13-18 min**	Varoma	

FOOD	AMOUNT	TIME	TM PART	TIPS AND TECHNIQUES
Asparagus	800 g	23-35 min	Varoma	• Time depends on thickness of stalks.
Peppers	100-300 g, cut in strips (1.5 cm)	10-14 min	Simmering basket	
	400-800 g, cut in strips (1.5 cm)	12-15 min	Varoma	
Button mushrooms	100-300 g, whole	10-15 min	Simmering basket	
	400-500 g, whole	15 min	Varoma	
	200-300 g, quartered	10-12 min	Simmering basket	• Cut large mushrooms in eighths.
	400-500 g, quartered	13-15 min	Varoma	
Peas	200-500 g, frozen	15-18 min	Simmering basket	
	600 g, frozen	18-22 min	Varoma	
New potatoes, small	600 g	30-35 min	Simmering basket	
	700-1200 g	35-40 min	Varoma	
Potatoes and sweet potatoes	200-600 g, cut in pieces (2-3 cm)	17-30 min	Simmering basket	
	700-1000 g, cut in pieces (2-3 cm)	20-35 min	Varoma	
Leeks	200-400 g, sliced	15-20 min	Simmering basket	
	500-800 g, sliced	20-25 min	Varoma	
Celery	200-400 g, cut in pieces (2 cm)	20-25 min	Simmering basket	
	500-800 g, cut in pieces (2 cm)	25-30 min	Varoma	
Celeriac	200-450 g, cut in pieces (2-3 cm)	13-17 min	Simmering basket	
	500-800 g, cut in pieces (2-3 cm)	20-25 min	Varoma	
Green beans	200-300 g, cut in pieces (3-5 cm)	15-25 min	Simmering basket	
	400-800 g, whole	15-30 min	Varoma	
Fennel bulbs	200-400 g, quartered	18-25 min	Simmering basket	
	500-800 g, quartered	27-30 min	Varoma	
	100-400 g, sliced (1 cm)	15-20 min	Simmering basket	
	500-800 g, sliced (1 cm)	18-25 min	Varoma	
Fresh spinach	500 g	10-12 min	Varoma	• Maximum 500 g.

FOOD	AMOUNT	TIME	TM PART	TIPS AND TECHNIQUES
Courgettes	200-500 g, halved, then sliced (1 cm)	**14-19 min**	Simmering basket	
	600-800 g, halved, then sliced (1 cm)	**20-25 min**	Varoma	

STEAMING FRUITS

FOOD	AMOUNT	TIME	TM PART	TIPS AND TECHNIQUES
Apples	200-400 g, quartered	**10-22 min**	Simmering basket	• Steaming time depends on variety and ripeness of apples.
	500 g, quartered	**12-25 min**	Varoma	• To double the quantity, insert Varoma tray and add a further 500 g.
Pears	200-400 g, quartered	**10-16 min**	Simmering basket	• Steaming time depends on variety and ripeness of pears.
	500-800 g, quartered	**15-20 min**	Varoma	
	200-400 g, halved	**13-18 min**	Simmering basket	
	500-800 g, halved	**18-23 min**	Varoma	
Apricots	300-400 g, halved	**9-12 min**	Simmering basket	• Steaming time depends on variety and ripeness of apricots.
	500 g, halved	**10-15 min**	Varoma	• To double the quantity, insert Varoma tray and add a further 500 g.
Peaches	300-450 g, halved	**8-12 min**	Simmering basket	• Steaming time depends on variety and ripeness of peaches.
	500 g, halved	**10-15 min**	Varoma	• To double the quantity, insert Varoma tray and add a further 500 g.
Plums	200-400 g, halved	**7-10 min**	Simmering basket	• Steaming time depends on variety and ripeness of plums.
	500 g, halved	**12-14 min**	Varoma	
Rhubarb	300-450 g, cut in pieces (1.5-2 cm)	**8-18 min**	Simmering basket	• Steaming time depends on variety and ripeness of rhubarb.
	500-800 g, cut in pieces (1.5-2 cm)	**12-22 min**	Varoma	• To make compote, sprinkle 400 g rhubarb in simmering basket with 80 g sugar and, without measuring cup (to avoid overboiling), steam **13-18 minutes**. For double the quantity, in Varoma dish, steam **17-20 minutes**. Transfer steamed rhubarb to a bowl, pour over the cooking liquid and leave to cool.

FOOD	AMOUNT	TIME	TM PART	TIPS AND TECHNIQUES
Pineapple	200-400 g, cut in triangles (5 mm thick)	**10-15 min**	Simmering basket	• Steaming time depends on variety and ripeness of pineapple. • To increase the quantity, insert Varoma tray and add a further 400 g.
	500 g, cut in triangles (5 mm thick)	**15-20 min**	Varoma	
Bananas with chocolate core	2 bananas, whole	**12 min**	Varoma	• Make a deep cut in the top of the banana and insert 1-2 pieces chocolate.
Papaya	1 small papaya, halved	**10-15 min**	Varoma	• To double the quantity, insert Varoma tray and add another papaya, halved.

STEAMING FISH AND SEAFOOD

FOOD	AMOUNT	TIME	TM PART	TIPS AND TECHNIQUES
Fish fillets (e.g. salmon, perch, bass, cod, haddock, snapper)	2-3 fillets (150 g each, 2-2.5 cm thick)	**12-18 min**	Varoma dish	• For frozen fish, increase steaming time by **5 min**.
	5-6 fillets (150 g each, 2-2.5 cm thick)		Varoma dish and Varoma tray	• To cook 5 fish fillets, place 2 in Varoma dish and 3 on Varoma tray.
Mussels, in the shell	500 g	**15 min**	Varoma dish	• Place mussels in Varoma dish. When water has reached Varoma temperature, place covered Varoma into position and steam.
	1000 g	**23 min**		• Take care when preparing mussels – gently tap on a work surface any that have open shells before cooking and discard any that do not close. Discard any mussels whose shell remains closed after cooking.
Large, raw prawns, with shell	400 g large prawns (40 g each), shell and head on	**9-11 min**	Simmering basket	• Ensure the prawns have turned pink and are fully cooked before removing.
	500 g large prawns (40 g each), shell and head on	**11-16 min**	Varoma dish	• For frozen prawns, increase time by **2 min**.
Whole fish (e.g. trout, bass, perch, bream, snapper)	2 (approx. 440 g)	**15-17 min**	Varoma tray	
	4 (approx. 440 g each)	**7-20 min**	2 in Varoma dish and 2 on Varoma tray	

STEAMING MEAT

FOOD	AMOUNT	TIME	TM PART	TIPS AND TECHNIQUES
Meatballs	500 g, apricot-sized	24-27 min	Varoma dish	
	1100 g, apricot-sized	24-27 min	500 g in Varoma dish and 600 g on Varoma tray	
Chicken breasts	3 breasts (approx. 500 g)	25 min	Varoma dish	• Make sure some holes remain unobstructed so that steam can circulate. • Place larger pieces in the Varoma dish, smaller pieces on the Varoma tray. • This time is for a well-done cooking result. Always ensure chicken is thoroughly cooked before serving.
	6 breasts (approx. 800 g)	25 min	2 in Varoma dish and 4 on Varoma tray	
Turkey escalopes	3 escalopes (approx. 600 g)	15-25 min	1 in Varoma dish and 2 on Varoma tray	• Make sure some holes remain unobstructed so that steam can circulate. • Always ensure turkey is fully cooked before serving.
Frankfurter sausages	6 sausages	10-15 min	Varoma dish	• Time depends on thickness of sausages.
	12-14 sausages	10-15 min	6 in Varoma dish and on Varoma tray	
Pork tenderloin	500 g, halved	25 min	Varoma dish	• Make sure some holes remain unobstructed so that steam can circulate. • Place larger pieces in the Varoma dish, smaller pieces on the Varoma tray. • This time is for a well-done cooking result. Ensure meat is thoroughly cooked before serving, with no pink meat visible.
	1500 g, halved	30 min	500 g (halved) in Varoma dish and 1000 g (halved) on Varoma tray	
Beef fillet	500 g (1 piece, whole)	12-30 min	Varoma dish	• Adjust steaming time to preferred level of doneness (longer for well-done meat). • For a delicious browned crust, briefly sear the fillet after steaming in a very hot non-stick frying pan and leave to rest for approx. 10 minutes wrapped in aluminium foil before serving.

Chapter Index

WEEKEND TIME

SPECIAL OCCASIONS

Alphabetical Index

P

Q

R

PHOTOGRAPHY / FOOD STYLING / ILLUSTRATION CREDITS

People and location photographs
Production executive: Esther Liesenberg
Art directors: Wiley Hoard, Dörte Nielsen,
Spring Agency Berlin
Photographer: Stefanie Aumiller
Location and clothes stylist: Katharina
Koppenwallner
Food styling: Xenia von Oswald, Sophie
von Oswald

Product photographs
Patric Eigermann

**All food photographs in the
introduction, editorials and
masterclasses, as well as all
TM6-exclusive recipe photos**
Photographer: António Nascimento,
Premier Picture Studio, Portugal
Art direction and styling: Ana Trancoso,
Premier Picture Studio, Portugal
Food styling: Cara Hobday, Catarina
Gouveia

Food photographs, other recipes
Photographer: Dennis Savini, Switzerland
Food styling: Judith Gmür-Stalder,
Switzerland

With the exception of
Pages 72, 73, 78, 92, 111, 114, 120, 175,
204, 208, 213 and 214
Photographer: Rob White
Food styling: Cara Hobday

Pages 42, 83, 146, 154, 155, 183, 206,
207 and 211
Photographer: Cristian Barnett
Food styling: Nicole Herft

Pages 77, 100, 101, 112, 180, 182, 193,
203 and 205
Photographer: Cristian Barnett
Food styling: Mima Sinclair

Pages 71, 104, 105, 115, 124, 145, 159
and 161
Photographer: Craig Kinder, f22
Photography, Australia
Food styling: Ursula Nairn, Australia

Pages 125, 130, 131, 132 and 156
Photographer: Cristian Barnett
Food styling: Hannah Yeadon

Pages 37, 102, 160, 163, 209 and 210
Photographer: Jacqui Melville
Food styling: Nicole Herft

Pages 74, 103 and 194
Photographer/Food Styling: Martin
Gentschow, Germany

Pages 75 and 136
Photographer: Antonio Forjaz
Nascimento, Portugal
Food styling: Ana Trancoso, Portugal

Pages 36 and 110
Photographer: Silvio Posada, Fernando
Merino, Spain

Page 44
Photographer: Dennis Savini, Switzerland
Food styling: Irène di Giacomo,
Switzerland

Page 70
Photographer: Bakerstreet SNC, Italy

Page 169
Photographer: Vorwerk Lux (Taiwan)

Page 202
Photographer: Cristian Barnett
Food styling: Vicki Smallwood

Page 215
Photographer: Alejandro Braña, Spain

Illustrations
Front cover, pages 15, 18 and 20
Marco Scuto, Italy
Page 29 Simone Andjelković, Germany

THANK YOU TO OUR TALENTED AND DEDICATED CONTRIBUTORS

We would like to thank everyone who contributed to the success of this project, in particular the editorial team and the recipe developers, for all the passion and hard work they dedicated to writing the editorial content and creating and improving the recipes. With our appreciation for their contribution.

IMPRINT

Project responsible overall
Francisco Cedillo

Marketing responsibles
Ramona Wehlig, José Namén

Inspiration and concept
Maria Resende

Editorial team
Cara Hobday, Editorial director,
Tasty Art, UK
Catarina Gouveia, Editorial director,
Portugal
Catarina Passos, Editor, Vorwerk Portugal
Irmgard Buth, Food consultant, Germany
Emma Plater, Editor, UK

Recipe development
Caroline Snook, Neil Lach-Szyrma, Libby
Millier, Teresa Peng
TM6 recipe development:
Catarina Gouveia, Conceição Coelho,
Maria Resende
TM6 recipe development technical
support:
Cara Hobday, Beatriz Rodríguez Diez,
Madalena Santos Lima, Christiane Stach
Resources tables: Evelin Guder
Recipes from The Basic Cookbook and
Great Taste on Every Level:
Corinna Haase

Project coordination
Astrid Carver-Courcier, Visual Explainer,
Switzerland

Nutritional values
Rebecca Dandy, UK
TM6 recipes: Angelika Ilies, Germany

Cookbook production
Concept/Design: Lichten, Germany
Design consultant: Stig Inge, STHEI,
Poland
Layout/typesetting: Effizienta oHG,
Germany

Photography and illustrations
See Photography/Food styling credits,
p. 250

Printing
Mohn Media, Germany

Edition/Publishing
1st Edition, June, 2019
11 languages

Editor
Vorwerk International & Co. KmG
Verenastrasse 39
8832 Wollerau
Switzerland

www.thermomix.vorwerk.co.uk

**Copyright© 2019 by
Vorwerk International & Co. KmG**
Text, design, photography, illustrations by
Vorwerk International & Co. KmG,
Switzerland.
All rights reserved.
This publication may not – in part or
whole – be reproduced, stored in a
retrieval system, recording or otherwise,
without the prior permission of
Vorwerk International & Co. KmG.

Article number: 25526 UK-en
ISBN: 978-3-03844-275-2